Naturally Supernatural

Regeneration

Anne Fundator

Author

Copyright © 2004 by Anne Fundator

Naturally Supernatural
by Anne Fundator

Printed in the United States of America

ISBN 1-594673-00-4

All rights reserved by the author. The contents and views expressed in this book are solely those of the author and are not necessarily those of Xulon Press, Inc. The author guarantees this book is original and does not infringe upon any laws or rights, and that this book is not libelous, plagiarized or in any other way illegal. If any portion of this book is fictitious, the author guarantees it does not represent any real event or person in a way that could be deemed libelous. No part of this book may be reproduced in any form without the permission of the author.

Unless otherwise indicated, Bible quotations are taken from the Holy Bible, New International Version. Copyright © 1973, 1978, 1984 by the International Bible Society. All rights reserved throughout the world. Used by permission of International Bible Society.

Acknowledgment

I give all thanks, praise, honor, and glory to Almighty God, Creator of the Universe. His great compassionate mercy and love exhibited through His Precious Son, my Savior and Lord, Jesus Christ, and the gentle leading of the Holy Spirit, inspired the writing of this testimonial booklet.

Table of Contents

Introduction

*T*he following synopsis may give you some insight in
your final analysis of why God so compassionately
manifested His glorious presence in my humble and broken
life.

I was born in the year 1919, a female child of immigrant
peasant farmers who were extremely devout Catholics. We
lived on a small farm during the Great Depression years.
(Just prior to the great Crash, my parents, who were living
in Chicago at the time, had fortunately withdrawn their meager savings from their bank and returned back East where
they had originally settled upon their arrival in America.)

During my early childhood years on the farm, Mother so
protected my sister and me that I hadn't the vaguest idea of
what was going on in the outside world other than through a
Sears Roebuck catalog. I never heard of the birds and bees
until I was seventeen years old. Life on the farm was rugged,
demanding, and backbreaking. My parents literally worked
themselves to death, and my sister and I had to work right
along with them to the extent of our strength also. Our only
source of income was derived from the monthly milk check,
which perhaps ranged from $15 to $50 per month during
peak seasons. Of course, we had an immense garden, which
supplied us with every vegetable imaginable. Fruit was plen-
tiful throughout the area; we picked and canned blackberries,

strawberries, etc., from various patches of state-owned lands within close proximity of our farm. Additionally, Mother made root beer for us, and we innocent, carefree children had the time of our lives. I might mention that my father also resorted to bootlegging and brewing beer to help supplement our meager income; he was jailed several times, but it did not stop him from doing it again when released.

Upon completion of my eighth grade education in a one-room schoolhouse adjacent to our property (first grade through eighth), the teacher had found a home for me in the nearby town where I worked throughout my high school years. Since no buses were provided by the school system to come back that far in the backwoods at that time, the only alternative was for me to leave the farm. Whether or not I was to attend high school was a constant heated debate; my father needed me on the farm, and my mother was determined that I was not going to be deprived of a high school education. When the appointed time arrived, Mother helped me escape by my crawling out of a bedroom window and racing to the nearest neighboring farmhouse. This, of course, had all been prearranged.

Upon being thrust into the beginning of the real world, I was deeply shocked and dismayed when I ultimately began to discover the haves and have nots; the dos and the don'ts; the good and the bad. My high school years were very trau-matic, and I endured many personal embarrassments; deep emotional scars were forming in my memory through taunt-ing humiliation inflicted upon me by some of the students because of my obvious naïveté, poverty, and nationality. Slowly and imperceptibly I began a progressive withdrawal from the cruelty of the world and deeply imbedded myself in reading, and because of my strict upbringing, only worth-while and educational material appealed to my tender, immature senses. For example, the most provocative book I ever read (I was just seventeen years old) was *Gone with the*

Wind. I vaguely remember somewhere along the way, when I was still in my teens, the book *Forever Amber* was placed in my hands. After reading ten or more pages of the novel (too much had not yet been developed of its theme), my conscience so strongly convinced me that it was immoral that I immediately threw it down like an ugly snake. I refused to read anything that was degrading throughout my adult life, and it never really was a temptation. How merciful was my Heavenly Father!

Upon graduating from high school, I found employment at what was then known as Hygrade Sylvania in the tiny town of Emporium, Pennsylvania. From there, the lure of the big city drew me to Buffalo, New York, where I worked at Bell Aircraft on the assembly line. The U.S. had already been attacked by Japan in 1941, and after a short time, my sister and I both entered the WAVES (the female branch of the Navy), after much urging from my mother.

During the time in the military, I developed several beautiful, sincere, and wonderful friendships with other WAVES. We couldn't understand the war, and we clung together as little children. Periodically, someone would receive tragic news of a dear friend, brother, father, sweetheart, fiancée, or husband, and we would uphold that person whose heart had been broken. Those were truly "bittersweet years." It was heartbreaking to daily witness the "cream of the crop" of our youngest and finest, beautiful young men going off to war, and so many of them knowing that perhaps they may never return. W.W.II was not a "hundred-day war"—Pearl Harbor 1941 was the beginning, and finally in 1945 the Americans and allies had brought Nazi Germany to her knees. Thousands of our American military lost their lives in all the battle areas of the war. As you can well imagine, our tender emotions during these years were racing from one extreme to another. We all were so very proud to be Americans. Parades and reviews were periodically scheduled for honorable dignitaries. For example, we did pass in review for then President Franklin D. Roosevelt. Every WAVE at Hunter College (Boot Camp)— six thousand, more or less—was in that parade. The Color Guard, leading the band itself, evoked heartfelt choking emotions of pride. The American flag does that to me and countless other loyal Americans as well. Unashamedly, tears of sorrow, joy, and pride would stream down my cheeks. Since I am a first-generation American, Mother taught us to be thankful, loyal citizens and to recognize how fortunate we were to have been born in America.

In order to bring cohesiveness to this work, this is perhaps an appropriate time to briefly outline events in my father's early life that might be of interest to you since it has a direct bearing on me. Specifically, was I "to be" or "not to be?" During his entire youth and early manhood, my father existed under the menacing cruelty and terror of the everspreading tentacles of that voracious monster, Russia, who was insidiously annexing, absorbing, etc., whole countries and segments of countries, one after another—Poland in this instance. My father joined a band of rebels; there were many such bands. These small pockets of resistance were futilely but bravely and courageously doing their best to voice their hatred of the tyranny inflicted upon them by Mother Russia. Alexander II (mid–1850s) did try to bring better reforms as he sensed a full-scale revolution was about to erupt, but he was assassinated in 1891. Nicholas II became Czar in 1894 (by that time my father had already arrived in America); Nicholas was the last Czar of Russia, and his final epitaph appropriately read, "Bloody Nicholas." I have read that unbelievably 100 million Russians, plus rebels such as my father, plus resisters from other countless surrounding countries, were murdered in the past two hundred years. Not a very pleasant history. And then Marxism began rearing its ugly head, and the embryonic rule of communism was born. My father was captured and deported to Siberia to a slave labor camp. He barely survived the ugly, unbelievable, and terrorizingly brutal internment. In several incredible series of events, he finally did escape before the turn of the century and safely made his way to America. My mother briefly explained to me the history regarding my father. I'm sorry I didn't care about learning more of his incredible life.

At the ripe old age of fourteen, I, too, was deported off to a nearby town to work for my bread and butter while attending high school. I rarely saw either of my parents except on certain holidays, etc. Since I could speak only a few basic words in Polish, and since my father could speak less English, communication was extremely limited in our relationship. Mother, however, studied diligently at learning basic English since she needed to be somewhat proficient to pass the exam for becoming a naturalized citizen. She was truly a most remarkable woman—she learned her English, however broken, and was ultimately sworn in as a U.S. citizen, the final fulfillment of her dearest childhood dream. You see, her father had also come to this amazing America long before she did; he worked faithfully in the lumber mills, amassed a small savings, returned to Poland, and related the glowing stories of the freedom and opportunity of this vibrant nation. When she reached fifteen or sixteen years of age, she implored her father to let her go to that fabulous America to seek her fortune. He finally gave in and financed her trip to America.

She had numerous stories to tell of the long trip across the big ocean (perhaps two weeks; I'm only guessing). Many were humorous, such as the incident when someone from First Class (noting that she was from Steerage) magnanimously gave her a banana. My mother did not know what it was or what to do with it. She had never seen one in her young life—not even a picture. When she found an opportune moment and when no one was around, with a great sigh of relief, she tossed it overboard. The ruling class prevented the peasants from becoming educated, and it was considered a criminal act if caught secretly teaching the children to read and write. She had what was equivalent to a third grade education, but she majored in human resourcefulness and finance. She brought the family through the Great Depression with her uncanny knowledge in handling and stretching the meager income of the family.

Upon my father's arrival in America, he settled in Austin, Pennsylvania, my birthplace—a tiny town in north central Pennsylvania that was happily and busily engaged in lumbering before the turn of the century. He was employed at the local paper mill, which was located perhaps a mile or more above the tiny town, peacefully nestled in the verdant valley, with majestic mountains rising on either side. About two miles above the mill, a dam had been proudly erected—a concrete dam, to replace the old earthen dam that was located approximately one mile above the site of the new structure. The town leaders felt that the old earthen dam should remain, as it would be a practical partial deterrent in the event of an unthinkable minor break in the new concrete dam until necessary repairs were made. Sadly, however, once the new structure began to give way on that fateful day, the earthen dam was completely obliterated. The forces of the break of the concrete dam literally sucked up the old dam into its rushing, violent, pent-up rage. It uprooted and ravaged everything in its path of terror as it crazily ricocheted from one side of the narrow valley to the other, racing onward to total destruction and death.

The civic leaders and promoters of the town's economy had determined that the concrete dam was the modern way to go. (We are talking eighty years ago.) The citizens were also in total agreement that construction was vitally necessary to provide the power to turn the wheels in the production of paper and its byproducts.

Upon its completion, the dam was proudly referred to as

"the dam that could not break," simply because they were assured they had the best engineers in the Northeast at that time masterminding this marvelous structure. This massive structure was 534 feet long and 43 to 50 feet high and was constructed in 1909. After its destruction, various estimates claimed it held 500 million gallons of water, more or less. The dam did attract hundreds of curious visitors (horse and buggy transport) from many miles away, which of course resulted in substantially promoting local businesses' cash flow, a nice big plus for the tiny town's economy. Tragically, within two short years, 1911, the dam that "could not break" did in fact give way, and the rest is history. It is estimated that eighty persons lost their lives; no doubt there were others who were unknown and undiscovered. Unfortunately, my father's first wife and little baby boy were also lost in the flood and were never located. Two of his older children survived. All the foregoing is to indicate that if the terrible tragedy had not occurred, I simply would not be here today. It is providentially apparent that I was destined to be born of the union of my widowed father, who now desperately needed a wife and mother to bring up his children, and my mother, who was only sixteen years old at that time, and who became his wife. It was in 1912, I believe. For me to have life, it was destined that his first wife tragically had to give up her life. The first miracle in this whole scenario was that my father escaped the deadly claws of the Russian Bear in Siberia. My birth was the second miracle (at least that's the way I feel about it). The third miracle of miracles was that thankfully I was born in America rather than Poland, Germany, or Russia (or any other country on the face of this earth).

As for the dam site itself, somewhere in its vicinity is an epitaph ruefully stating "how not to build a dam." For some poignant and compelling reason, I find myself frequently visiting the dam site and spending quiet time and meditation over the great evidence of what eighty years can do to an uninhabited structure. The town, which to me as a child seemed to be large and exciting, is now only a feeble ghost town with a small number of senior residents remaining. The old remains of the concrete dam still exist, however, but as a bizarre, contorted, grotesque effigy on concrete visibly reflecting the excruciating agony it had experienced as the awesome raging power of the released, pent-up, deceivingly silent waters brutally and savagely destroyed it forever back in 1911.

Now returning to my high school years, and away from the safety of the nest during the crucial years when I most needed parental guidance, I made countless tragic, traumatic mistakes. But since I was endowed with the peasant blood-line stock and the dogged perseverance of my parents, I kept plugging on. Somehow throughout all the blunders, I knew God was somewhere, and even though I called out to Him repeatedly, I had not been able to make contact. Nonetheless, He was always present in my silent thoughts, and I wondered how, when, and where He would ultimately reveal Himself to me.

Finally, at the age of fifty-one, when I had lived life "my way"—the foolish way—it all dynamically began to come together. I gently and earnestly urge you to grasp this opportunity, perhaps the only opportunity some of you will ever have, to open the door, walk in, and be introduced to King Jesus in a supernatural manner. Please make yourself comfortable—spend several hours with me as we together explore the exciting realm of the real world (the invisible world)—*and know that it can happen to you too!*

Addendum 1992

For your information, my original manuscript was completed and copyrighted in 1981.

Swiftly and with lightning speed, eleven years have passed since my original manuscript was completed and copyrighted. After shelving the then entitled *Beautifully Born Again* manuscript, and in what appeared to be a suspension of time, I do believe the Lord wanted me to grow and mature to better update certain areas of the 1981 edition. This to me emphatically indicates the leading of the Holy Spirit. It was also during this suspended time period that I felt the need to change the title to *Naturally Supernatural*. As you continue on, you will discover why I did. Try to remember one thing: God is never in a hurry, even when we are. And remember it takes time to grow—lots and lots of time—especially spiritual growth. The loud and clear message I received was that I am to quote scripture verses rather than just naming to you, the reader, the Book, chapter, and verse. Possibly many of you do not even own a Bible. If you read this book from start to finish, I truly believe one of the first purchases you will make is a copy of the Holy Bible, even perhaps before you finish *Naturally Supernatural*. Additionally, there are several incidents of fulfillment providing stronger clarification and credibility of God's Word to you who are earnestly seeking. Remember that I am now eleven years older spiritually, and I have a more mature perception as a result of the eleven-year developing time factor.

This final phase of the Introduction gives the readers events that explain exactly how, why, and where this book was written. You will discover an orderly progression of situations leading up to my employment as Mansfield State College and beyond, where I spent ten years (quite educational, I must say) as the secretary to the director of the Computer Educational Center (CEC). During the tenure of the second director and the last five years of my employment, an occasion arose whereby our government was seeking persons of the highest level of computer expertise available in the U.S. to attend a conference in Europe. In response, my director's highly technical work was submitted to the agency, and she was selected on the basis of her technical expertise in the field of computers. I don't know exactly how many others were selected from the U.S.—but additionally, other VIPs were chosen from the Big Three Nations as well as other smaller developing nations. Needless to say, they comprised an "enormous think tank" of unparalleled computer geniuses at that time. The conference was scheduled for six or seven workdays in Vienna, Austria. After the conference, all went their separate ways.

Back to my boss, it would be inappropriate not to mention that she has worked on modeling projects ranging from analytical mathematical integration at Columbia University to modeling operations of a Polaris submarine at Vitro Laboratories. She received her M.Sc. in mathematics from the Courant Institute of Mathematical Science at New York University. Furthermore, before she left the college, her book, *Structured System Analysis: A New Technique*, was published by Gordon and Breach, London, New York, and Paris. (We worked on that book for approximately one year.) Needless to say, I was mentioned in her Acknowledgment along with three of her colleagues for their assistance and insights to her theories. And to think I served as her secretary! For that alone I feel very honored indeed!

With the boss away, I thought it was going to be a bonus vacation time for me since the producer of the work volume would be in Vienna and I could just enjoy the let-up of the constant pressure. However, my vacation never began, since through the gentle but persistent leading of the Holy Spirit, in some supernatural way I began to sense that I must type my version and understanding of my glorious new birth. Customarily as each day began, and the wheels of education began to revolve, I would dutifully and efficiently perform the routine chores of the office. These included answering dozens of phone calls and responding to constant interruptions of students who worked part-time in the CEC as well as CEC professors just popping in to discuss schedules for upcoming student exams and my availability to do the typing. During the ten days of her absence, and by typing 85 to 100 words per minute (wpm), observers said that my typewriter literally was smoking—ha, I like that—the first draft of *Naturally Supernatural* was completed. Of course, I did on several occasions remain after office hours to work on the manuscript. All in all, perhaps I spent fifty hours, more or less, on the first draft.

Obviously, at that time, I really had no idea of why I was doing it. But the Holy Spirit knew. It's no big secret that as the years pass by, our memories do tend to slow down, and many events simply fade away. I do believe with all my heart that God wanted me to record the wonderful miracles that had taken place in my early new birth years and to share them with you before it all becomes a beautiful but less vivid memory. I'm so thankful I was obedient to the gentle nudging of the Holy Spirit. God has revealed from the beginning of time that nothing is impossible for Him (just look at His glorious creation of earth and outer space, as well as Man, His masterpiece). The Lord Jesus will be delighted to lead and guide you in every aspect of your life if you will but ask Him to enter in and be Lord over your life. His workings are unfathomable and beyond all human understanding. Take this moment, right now, and truly repent of your sins verbally, ask forgiveness of those sins, and then thank Jesus and ask Him to come into your heart and be Lord over your life. It's truly that simple! Then stand back in childlike faith in wonder, meekness, and humbleness as He begins to unfold His awesome will by revealing a marvelous purpose, tailored only for your particularly unique life.

Finally, to neatly conclude this Introduction and to bring home several points, can you not see that if my boss providentially had not been one of the chosen VIPs for the Vienna visit, just possibly this book would not have been written at that specific point in time? Of course, our Great Creator would simply have engineered another exciting scenario to fulfill His divine purpose, known only to Him, however obscure it may seem to you and me at the moment. The past twenty years of my life have been divinely sustained by His ever-glorious Presence that constantly envelops and encourages me to keep on going no matter what.

I now humbly pray to my Heavenly Father that everyone who reads this Holy Spirit–inspired book will be blessed with unending hope, love, and joy; to face life bravely and honorably; and to ever acknowledge openly and publicly that Jesus, the Son of God and Second person of the Divine Trinity, came to earth to die in our place for the sins we are guilty of, to reveal the Father, and to reconcile us with the Father. Study the Bible diligently so that you may truly be called the "sons and daughters" of God through the constant unfolding irrefutable evidence of your new birth. Yes, there must be positive evidence exhibited in your day-to-day existence that you really have supernaturally been *"born again!"* Alleluia and Alleluia.

After all is said and done, there is only one *primary* purpose of this Holy Spirit–inspired work, and that is to bring as many souls as possible to the understanding of the new birth. So now, *before* you begin the first chapter, "Beautifully Born Again," won't you prayerfully, in ordinary language, simply ask the Holy Spirit to give you understanding, peace, and joy as you read through this miracle book? God will surely bless you as you earnestly seek to enter His Glorious Kingdom.

Anne Fundator

Chapter 1

Beautifully Born Again

*B*orn again! There it is again. This mysterious and tantalizing expression is being echoed around the world, reverberating louder and louder, over and over again. What exactly does it mean? Let's see what the Author of life has to say about it in His Word taken from the Gospel of John 3:1–8. Nicodemus, a member of the Jewish ruling council, came to Jesus at night to question as well as to affirm his belief that Jesus was a teacher from God because of the marvelous signs He was performing. Jesus declared, "I tell you the truth, no one can see the kingdom of God unless he is born again." Nicodemus questioned, "How can a man be born when he is old? Surely he cannot enter a second time into his mother's womb to be born!" Jesus answered, "I tell you the truth, no one can enter the kingdom of God unless he is born of water and the Spirit. Flesh gives birth to flesh, but the Spirit gives birth to spirit. You should not be surprised at my saying, 'You must be born again.' The wind blows wherever it pleases. You hear its sound, but you cannot tell where it comes from or where it is going. So it is with everyone born of the Spirit."

Many versions, varieties, and volumes of books written on born again experiences have been marketed and proclaimed; however, it simply cannot be understood by anyone outside the phenomenon unless the interested individual is willing to listen, act, and then experience it. These two words mean just what they say: you are born again—truly, gloriously, regenerated within your spirit. All born again experiences are excitingly unique (just as you are unique). I've heard hundreds of testimonies, some exceptionally dramatic, some sweetly sublime, and some seemingly of no visible or tangible consequence whatsoever at the "moment" of regeneration (comparable to a tiny newborn baby who has no idea of its existence for some time). Yet "something incredible" has happened: the spark of life has now been energized by the Holy Spirit. And this energized spark must be constantly nourished by daily, consistent study of the Word of God—daily vitamins for the spirit. Neglect would prove to be disastrous to that new born again child, resulting in stunted growth and development to maturity.

Everyone seeking and embracing the born again experience will meet our Savior, and that meeting is incomparable in revealing the exquisite, holy essence of Christ Jesus. Surprisingly, you do immediately recognize something supernatural has occurred, but ultimately there is initial evidence of the budding of the fruits of the Spirit beginning to develop. Bearing the mature fruits of the Spirit does take some time, however, and these fruits are love, joy, peace, patience, goodness, kindness, faithfulness, gentleness, and self-control. If you have truly been regenerated, these fruits will begin to appear and will become a natural part of your life without even trying. The simple statement of "by their fruits you shall know them" is indeed a profound fact, and the visible irrefutable consequence is ultimately reflected in the life of a truly born again person. Sadly, many Christians say they are born again, but their lifestyles are a dead give-away that they are deluding themselves entirely. Your life becomes a startling, visible testimony to the doubter, and incidentally, to you as well.

How does one begin to try and explain to an unbeliever that something divinely orchestrated actually happens to a person earnestly seeking God? Do you think for a moment that your Heavenly Father will deny revealing Himself to you when you, in childlike faith, earnestly seek His Presence; to really know Him in some way that would some-how begin to satisfy the ever yearning, something missing, void within your soul—or really not knowing what you are longing to know? No more than you would deny yourself to your own child. Unbelievers turn deaf ears; they ridicule; they ever so subtly persecute the child of God; some are very hostile; they are coldly indifferent; they are just not inter-ested; and it is written, ultimately they may kill you because you know the Truth. What is Truth? Truth is Jesus Christ. John 14:6: "Jesus answered, 'I am the way and the truth and the life. No one comes to the Father except through me.'"

There comes a day when the unbeliever will honestly admit and recognize within the depths of his soul that he sim-ply doesn't want a change in his self-dominated lifestyle. He is afraid he will have to give up earthly, material posses-sions—visible things. He won't be able to adjust to a new life; he is somewhat pacified with this life, unfulfilling though it may be. Actually, he is in a rut and too listless to try to get out. Whatever in this world could possibly be more exciting than learning about the Author of Life, the Creator of the universe, the awesome power mysteriously holding the universe together? God is the Creator, the Creator of everyone and everything seen and unseen; however, after being spiritually revived, regenerated, born again, you are His spiritual child, and He is now your Spiritual Father. Now you can communicate with Him as Father and child. But before you are born again, and your spirit is dead, you simply cannot communicate with a Spiritual Creator. Oil and water simply do not mix. Now you are a flesh child born of the flesh. Jesus said, "You must be born again of the Spirit" (John 3:5–8). Unregenerate, you simply don't understand, and in perplexity you appease yourself into accepting this hollow, shadowy existence. No amount of "material possessions" can satisfy the secret yearning within your soul. You are literally "bogged down" in the futile flow of day-to-day drudgery. Why don't you resolve right now to give yourself half a chance to know your Creator? Actually, when you know God, you won't have to "give up" anything; on the contrary, you will begin to receive from Him. Primarily and of supreme importance, you are now the possessor of eternal life in the glory hereafter for all eternity; can you possibly compare this to any earthly treasure? Of course you cannot.

As you begin to take root in this newfound knowledge, you will begin to prioritize your desires, and the gentle Holy Spirit will assist you if you allow Him. God will gently and lovingly cause you to begin to release the desires of the perishable, the tawdry, the tinsels you once cherished, good or bad, and in return will reward you with an insatiable, earnest desire to seek His will and the indefinable, unfolding glories of His Truth for you *now, here on earth.* Slowly you begin to recognize a partial, fragile fulfillment, and the nagging void within begins to subside. Finally, the everlasting priorities are set up. Since you have made this wisest of wise decisions, earthly priorities are unregrettably relinquished and finally laid to rest. You really don't give up anything of value, but you do begin to glimpse and understand the grand panorama of life in its truest meaning, and day by day as you earnestly and fervently seek God, wisdom and knowledge are graciously imparted to you. All born again experiences are selectively unique and you, too, will sense the wisdom of your great God to give each of us an experience as diversely different as we are from each other. No carbon copies here. Some born again experiences are quite dramatic and others are gently sublime; however, whatever the experience, you will wisely know it is of divine origin. You become an "open book" for the world to read. You are a light in a dark world. However, above all, do not expect an overnight miracle of some magical transformation of your being; this is just the beginning of your earthly spiritual existence. As you apply yourself with the knowledge being unfolded to you as you diligently study the Bible, the Sword of the Spirit, you amazingly begin to grow and grow within your spirit. You begin to receive knowledge of the reality of God's plan in this life just for you. Before the born again experience, you could not communicate with God because He is Spirit and you are flesh. Your spirit becomes alive after you ask the Lord Jesus to become Lord of your life and to ask Him to live within your heart; then and only then, and after sincere repentance, this miracle of miracles can take place. Then you are born again and you begin to understand how to communicate with God. Unregenerate, you are baffled, you cannot begin to understand what life is really all about, you feel you really don't care, and you abjectly accept your lifestyle. Won't you give yourself a chance to see just who you are when you are *regenerated* and you are no longer just a *natural* run-of-the-mill human being—you are *supernatural*? This spiritual potential power within you is unlimited and awesome in its scope.

Understandably, now you have no curiosity about the supernatural life because you are dead—not physically, but spiritually. You are bogged down in the affairs of everyday death. You're not really alive yet—not until you have repented of your sins and accepted Jesus as Lord over your life. After the born again experience, earthly things amazingly diminish in importance; you wonder why on earth you ever thought they were important. These trite, meaningless desires you now exchange for riches that never decay; you now have the divine privilege of coming into the Presence of Almighty God—a magnificent, awesome God to be adored and worshipped. We are created in His image. Just try to digest those simple but profound words for several days, and you will discover the pitiful, earthly beggar you are and thus far have chosen to be. By remaining a resister, an unbeliever, you are spiritually dead and destined for everlasting hell removed from the Presence of Almighty God.

Unbelievers ridicule our claims of having the divine experience of meeting our Lord and Savior of the world. Ah, my heart is truly in pain for them. The higher educated non-believers are the most obstinate to approach and are dead to communicating anything but the "scientific." No number of college degrees could ever satisfy the truly intelligent mind. Education seemingly is a myth; it is a mockery and never really solved any of the sicknesses of the soul or the down-to-earth problems of the world such as hunger, poverty, crime, drugs, etc. Various and sundry degrees are merely an exercise in mind expansion. Anyone given the opportunity can learn from a book, and without wisdom to apply knowledge, intelligence is null and void. Not everyone can know the deepest secrets of the universe unless he first seeks the Creator of that universe; born again believers begin to receive wisdom from God for living in this complex, perplexing life.

The so-called intellectual merely touches the surface of the unfathomable universe in his short-circuited mind. At a point in time, he recognizes the vast, infinite mystery of the universe—and because he cannot fully understand it, measure it (he keeps trying), or reduce it to his finite understanding, he literally blows his fuse. And there he sits, forevermore hamstrung by his so-called intellect. Is it any wonder that many of the so-called literates have resorted to ultimately destroying themselves? There they were almost at the door of revelation—but stubbornly refused to take a step forward, open the door, and enter in. Ah, the terrible destructive enemy of man: intellectual pride. Man must acknowledge first of all that there is someone greater than he; otherwise he cannot be reached. This is similar to an alcoholic—unless he admits he is an alcoholic, he cannot be assisted. But pride and intellect get in the way; pride is the murderer of man—the downfall of millions. And the terrible tragedy is that the brain expansionists are forever instilling and trying to instill in the minds of the spiritually dead the degrading fallacy of evolution and the ape, his father. What you say is what you are—so be it. But as for me, I am created in God's image. All manner of cross-breeding within the same species has been generally accepted by man, but I wonder how God feels about it. Man has proven over and over again that he cannot be satisfied—that is, until he is born again. There is no point in crossing over the boundaries; you see it nakedly expressed before your eyes—man wants to be God. Man didn't get far with breeding the horse and donkey, did he? Two closely related animals, first cousins you might say, were bred and produced a sterile animal; isn't that what so-called interfacing and evolution are all about? The end product is compared to a sterilized mule. I dread to see what the scientists must be doing behind locked doors to prove their theory of the evolution of man—and here we have the answer in God's Word. "And God said, Let the earth bring forth the living creature *after his kind,* cattle, and creeping thing, and beast of the earth *after his kind:* and it was so. And God made the beast of the earth *after his kind,* and cattle *after their kind,* and every thing that creepeth upon the earth *after his kind:* and God saw that it was good" (Genesis 1:24–25 kjv, emphasis added).

Man is trying his intellectual utmost to deny God—and his own plans have defeated his ignoble purposes. The result compares to the breeding of a horse and donkey, which produces a sterile male. The man who enforces the teaching of evolution as scientific truth is already condemned to a horror of eternal damnation, not necessarily because he is teaching a theory of evolution but because he is blatantly and callously shutting God out of the picture. Recently, however, it is being disclosed that more and more scientists are abandoning their original dogmatic theories of evolution (and I believe with much relief) because they have discovered gross error in the theory of one man. (Incidentally, did you know that Darwin, upon his deathbed, was embracing the Holy Bible?)

Every person knows inherently that God *is* the Creator of this fantastic universe. The pride of man arrogantly chooses to cast aside and stifle that inborn ray of light. That one is guilty of trying to pervert the mind of God's highest creation—man—and dragging others to hell with him. God does not accept that. As for me, I am created in God's image. "God said, Let us make man in our image [the Trinity], after our likeness [man consists of spirit, soul, and body]: and let them have dominion over the fish of the sea, and over the fowl of the air, and over the cattle, and over all the earth, and over every creeping thing that creepeth upon the earth. So God created man in his own image, in the image of God created he him; male and female created he them" (Genesis 1:26–27 kjv). God said it, and I choose to believe it.

Unbelievers think that if you can't see it, feel it, smell it, taste it, and hear it, it doesn't exist, and if you can't put it in a test tube and bubble it up, it isn't so. Yet, paradoxically, they know there is more unseen in this world than seen because the unseen (reality) produces the seen: electricity, sound waves, atoms, wind, etc., ad infinitum. The resulting expression of these unseen things is the matchless, incomparable rhythm and harmony of the universe. The rotation of the earth creating the seasons, the rising and setting of the sun, the tides, the moon, and all the planets, known and unknown, in their orbits, are all commanded to perform by the Word of God. The power of His Word is what upholds the precise stabilization and impeccable order of the entire universe.

The dynamic born again experience (mine) enriches my life to the fullest extent of human understanding of the role of God and the universe. Now I will reveal to you several incredible scenes of the so-called unseen world that God so lovingly opened my spiritual eyes to see—the supernatural, the spiritual realm. They are absolutely boggling to my mind! This will be just a tiny peek, mind you, since at this stage, God in His infinite wisdom knew that my mind couldn't absorb any more than was revealed to me. God is so wonderful. He absolutely delights in taking a humble person (He very seldom works with arrogant beings) who has soulfully searched (not scientifically) and at last discovered the reality of an Almighty Creator. He is the Creator who controls our every breath, the very destiny of our fleeting moment of earthly existence (as compared to eternity), and magnanimously begins to impart wisdom according to His will to that searching child of His and begins to unfold the unending mysteries of the universe.

At this point, I must explain that I have been somewhat impatient waiting for the Holy Spirit to convince me that *now* is the time to reveal some of my spiritual experience to those of you who are reading this book—those of you who are resistant doubters but nonetheless are intuitively knowledgeable of the fact that "there must be something more" because as I have stated, God imparts to everyone that ray of knowledge of His deity. How does a person transmit on paper the other dimension: the spiritual realm? This is a challenging mountain for me to scale (remember I am just a baby in spirit)—but with the power and leading of the Holy Spirit (my Teacher) and the wisdom God imparts to me, I will find the proper words to convey what I am delighted to share with you—the basic beginner; the reluctant, doubting seeker. It isn't all easy. Many times in the past eight years since I was gloriously born again, I have wanted to get up on any soapbox and shout all about my new acquaintance with God. However, I simply was not sufficiently mature in the Spirit and would not be a credible witness of God's dealing in my life. Our spiritual growth depends upon our spiritual food: the Holy Bible. As I am learning, the fruits of the Spirit must begin to blossom, determined only by my understanding of the Word of God. As we all know, fruits harvested too early are not edible. God has restrained my longing most of the time, but occasionally I escaped His watchful eyes (I thought), climbed out of the playpen, and fell flat on my face. Those dear brothers and sisters in Christ who were actually trying to help me clipped my tiny sprouting wings. They knew the Word, but I did not. I was too green. But thank God that I am now beginning to ripen, and He can now use me as He wills.

So, my dear readers, this is a message of hope to those of you who are confused about the future—your future after death. To eliminate the doubt, the fear of death, and the consequences to follow, you must accept the plan of salvation God has provided us in accepting His Son to cleanse us from sin. Christ Jesus took all of our sins within Himself on Calvary's cross, and in exchange gave us HIS righteousness if we chose to accept Him. There is no other way for man to be saved except through the blood of Christ. Acts 4:12 states, "Salvation is found in no one else, for there is no other name under heaven given to men by which we must be saved." Also, Romans 1:16–17 states, "I am not ashamed of the gospel, because it is the power of God for the salvation of everyone who believes: first for the Jew, then for the Gentile. For in the gospel a righteousness from God is revealed, a righteousness that is by faith from first to last, just as it is written: 'The righteous will live by faith.'" And Hebrews, Chapter 5:8–10 states, "Although he was a son, he learned obedience from what he suffered and, once made perfect, he became the source of eternal salvation for all who obey him and was designated by God to be high priest in the order of Melchizedek." Keep in mind, however, that true and sincere repentance of your sins is absolutely imperative along with confession that Jesus is God's Son before any regeneration of your spirit can take place. I must repeat: if you are not truly repentant and remember Almighty God knows your heart, regeneration will not take place; you will be deluded into thinking you are saved when actually you are not. That is extremely dangerous—like playing Russian roulette. I know of one incident in particular. A person was not one hundred percent ready to submit his total life to the Lord Jesus and went through the motions anyway. God knew his heart was not totally yielded to Jesus, and sadly, salvation did not take place. This is not a game you are playing—this is forever. If you think you can put on a front, go through the motions, and still have access to the glorious throne of our Holy God, you are dead wrong. Examine yourself again, approach other believers for counsel, prepare yourself again for the "finals," and with *true* repentance, confess your sins to Jesus, ask forgiveness, and ask Him to enter your heart, and you can be assured He will.

And I am assured from His Word, as I continue to diligently study, that spiritual growth is ever constant and growing. Studying the Holy Word of God is the prime requisite of truly knowing what God is saying to us. It has been quoted: "Those who have grown in grace are the very ones to whom He reveals still more." After my glorious conversion, I spent four or five hours each night for approximately five years studying the Word. No radio, television, or going out—nothing but study. Amazingly, I didn't want anything else except to know my Creator and Savior more intimately, and the only way I could accomplish this was to study His Word! You simply cannot understand the Bible if you are not born again; the Bible is God's Word to man, and He inspired devout men by His Holy Spirit to write it. Only spiritually born again persons can begin to understand the Bible as they apply themselves. If you are not a regenerated being, you are a natural being. Therefore, when you become a spiritually regenerated person, it is only natural that you will begin to experience the spiritual world because you are now a supernatural person with the Holy Trinity residing within you. If you are interested in knowing Almighty God, the supernatural, *then dig in!* There is no other way. That is the secret of intimate communion with God as you seek Him in prayer. That is when He manifests Himself to you, during your prayer and praise and thanksgiving time. I could not be of use to God until I knew His Word. And the more I study, the more it is revealed to me that it's not totally *what you do,* but what your relationship is to God. He yearns for our love and devotion first, and then comes service. Then a mind-boggling revelation of His plans begins to emerge in our lives now and for eternity. A never-ending gold mine of spiritual riches is there for those who patiently and lovingly seek *Him* in this life by obediently studying His Word.

What continually astounds me is the fact that people in this entire universe daily exhibit "faith" in every imaginable aspect of life. For instance, you let the doctor inject you with medication, to slice and chop you up into mincemeat, to remove a few goodies from your body, and to poke and probe in every conceivable way throughout your body. You get into your auto or someone else's or you get into an airplane, exhibiting a form of "faith," like it or not. Now it was through your own will you did those things. Through necessity you are forced to accept the offered modes of travel; when your life is in jeopardy, you gladly accept the advice of your physician. What in this world could be more crucial than accepting "by faith" the fact that Jesus Christ, by His death and resurrection, gave you the option of where you will spend eternity? You have nothing to lose and eternal life to gain. What is preventing you from accepting Jesus by faith? When you do, I can assure you that God Himself will begin to work in your heart and reveal to you what His entrance into your life will mean. The Holy Spirit will begin to reveal to you the meaning of the words of Almighty God—incredibly, you will now begin to grasp spiritual understanding, you will be overwhelmed, and you will be assured of salvation. And all it takes is the same faith you exhibit every day of your life under various circumstances. Try it—you have nothing to lose—and enter with love into the presence of Almighty God through His Glorious Son, our Savior, Jesus Christ. You see, you can check this out for yourself. But until you do, be careful how you think of us, God's redeemed children.

All those who tragically want to know about alcohol, drugs, smoking, etc. *try it out first,* don't they? They don't just listen to someone describe the experience. They go ahead and experience it for themselves. How can you possibly know there is or is not something else unless you prove it to yourself, and how can you prove or disprove it unless you search it out? That is the only way you can know what we are talking about. Stop knocking it and prove us wrong. You do not have to be in an audience. But it's better to have a witness, just as you have witnesses when you are married. You can be on your knees in your own bedroom—or anywhere, for that matter. (This may not be pertinent, but somewhere I read about Jerry Lewis' wife, a born again Christian. She was in a plane over the Atlantic Ocean thirty-five thousand feet in the air when she asked Jesus to baptize her with His Holy Spirit so she would have the necessary power to live for Him in her most troubled time. God did baptize her with the evidence of speaking in a new language.)

There is only one way into eternal life, and that is through faith in Jesus Christ. Jesus said, "I am the way, the truth, and the life: no man cometh unto the Father, but by me" (John 14:6 kjv). There is *no other way.* No one with an IQ either under 100 or over 100 can risk the consequences—it is too horrible. So you see, in summation, all it takes is to kneel on your pride and bring it to its knees. Remember I mentioned earlier that pride is a murderer. Bring this murderer to its knees. In all humbleness and faith, ask God to save your soul by your confession of belief in Jesus Christ, by accepting Him as your Lord and Savior, and from that very moment you will inherit eternal life. Then as you submit your will to the Holy Spirit, He will begin to teach you as you diligently study the Word and now begin to receive an understanding of the whole spectrum of life. You are now a new creature, born again spiritually unto everlasting life in the glorious Kingdom of God. Praise His holy name as you resolve to continue your walk with Him.

Chapter 2

Meeting the Incomparable Kathryn Kuhlman

I had been living in Phoenix, Arizona, since 1967, after escaping from an ugly, intolerable marital situation that was destroying my will to live. It was so bad, in fact, that at one time I took a bottle of aspirin to try to end it all. Of course, it only put me to sleep for three days, three heavenly days of rest, which I desperately needed. I was very interested in life in its fullest meaning, but unfortunately, because of being deprived of my mother's counsel during my teen years, I knew very little of anything. I am not stupid, nor was I closed to the search for truth. In fact, I desperately hungered to know the truth just as a scientist hungers to solve whatever he is pursuing at the moment. I was temporarily living with a dear friend I had known while living in Chicago and who had moved to Arizona earlier. Her husband was a surveyor for the state and was away from home five days a week. Needless to say, we had a marvelous reunion since I hadn't seen her for four or five years. During my stay with her, roughly three months, she began to introduce me to teachings on ESP, Area for Research and Enlightenment (ARE), reincarnation, astrology, yoga, and Edgar Cayce (the Sleeping Prophet) philosophies. Cayce was extremely interesting, but as I must in all fairness question some of my spiritual revelations, I must also fairly question the source of his revelations. I was interested somewhat, but I *never* doubted my belief in God and the Most Holy Trinity—God the Father, God the Son, and God the Holy Spirit. I attended several meetings and listened to various tapes about the above-mentioned topics, but my faith was never shaken—and I wasn't even born again at that time. God works in such mysterious, exciting ways, since it was through her that I came to know Jesus, my wonderful Savior. She believed Jesus was in the world at one time, and that He lived and died, but she did not believe she would have everlasting life by believing that He was indeed the Son of God who obediently came into the world to ransom all sinners who choose to be ransomed.

Ultimately, this dear friend informed me (after I had my own apartment) of a Christian service to be held in Phoenix with the speaker Kathryn Kuhlman, an evangelist of some renown who supposedly had the "gift of healing." Right here let me tell you that Miss Kuhlman reiterated over and over again that she did not have the power of healing—only God does—but she, as a born again believer, became a living vessel (catalyst) for God to work through. God needs all of us; we are extensions of His hands and voice. My dear friend had an adopted son who was eighty-five percent blind, but she, in faith—here we go: she in "faith"—was going to take her son to that meeting for a possible healing of her son's sight, and she urged me to go to the meeting also. Another friend and I took her up on it. What did I have to lose?

Nothing—absolutely nothing. What did I have to gain? Everything—my life, in fact. Well, needless to say, her son's eyesight was not restored, but there were many who in faith believed and received and were healed. Through this seemingly casual adventure, God was sovereignly making arrangements for me to be introduced to His Son. So here we have it in a nutshell. I was a Catholic; my friend was a Gentile (not a Christian), but she was hoping to receive healing for her child through someone she did not believe in. Generally, that just doesn't add up. You cannot add apples and sugar. (However, our Omnipotent God can and does do the impossible whenever and however He wills, and for whatever purpose known only to Him.)

The day of the meeting arrived, and my dear friend, Lois, and I decided to attend. We entered the jam-packed building and found two seats. At the scheduled time, Miss Kuhlman made her entrance amidst resounding applause. My, what a marvelous creation! She looked like an angel. Her gown was floor-length, flowing, and white with a mandarin collar and gold-cuffed sleeves. What captivated me completely was her ethereal radiance. Reader, you know something—true Christianity is vibrant, light, clean, fragrant, and good. When Jesus approached the men who were to become His disciples, He would say to them, "Come, follow me," and they dropped everything because they were irresistibly drawn to His person. Miss Kuhlman is an excellent example of a true Christian in every sense of the word. She radiated goodness, literally. C'mon, let's face it: most of us (with spiritual discernment) can detect a moral person— she was far more than that. It was beautiful the way the service unfolded. She led us in singing for perhaps fifteen to twenty minutes—a very high form of praising God. It was an atmosphere in which the Holy Spirit was worshipped and adored and in which He would manifest His omnipotent power. She referred to scripture, commenting on it; she talked to the audience; and she was exuberant, radiant, humorous, and above all, most natural. People were getting into the "spirit" of the meeting. They were thinking good things; praising God in song; and praying for healing of the soul, mind, and whatever body afflictions they might have. Each person in his own way was trying to contact the divine source that would bring him healing, physically or spiritually or both. She continued in the Word. Since the majority of us were Christian—however weak and frail—we began to understand that she was teaching us (in spite of ourselves) the working of the Holy Spirit. Finally came the climax— she sensed through her heart (ah, there we have it—the heart, the presence of the Holy Spirit), she was prompted by the Holy Spirit to indicate certain persons in the audience who would receive something from God. She mentioned afflictions, a multitude of diseases; she pointed toward those persons with certain ailments as being healed at that moment by the power of the Holy Spirit.

This incredible scene continued for perhaps three hours. I was amazed; I believed and yet I didn't want to believe a word of what I was witnessing. (Does that sound like you?) People by the hundreds had been healed. There was much rejoicing, laughter, and prayers of thanksgiving—amens and hallelujahs. I heard "Praise the Lord" and "Thank you, Jesus," over and over again. Now if you had received a healing, wouldn't you want to tell everyone that God healed you? Of course you would. Tell me, what do you do when your favorite football team scores a seemingly impossible touchdown? I know what you do because once upon a time I was wild about pro football. I would pound and shout, and I would shout and pound anyone within pounding distance. I would be fanatically screaming for our team until I lost my voice. Well, so do we as born again Christians become avid fans—I am one of the fanatics for Jesus. I can't help myself and don't intend to—He saved my soul from the fires of hell. Now that is something to shout about. Don't you agree?

At the close of the service, all the people healed had the opportunity to go on stage and tell the audience about how they were miraculously healed. There were approximately twenty-five hundred of us at that meeting in May of 1971. Miss Kuhlman would question the individual who professed to having been healed, and after she was convinced within her spirit of the person's healing, she would raise her hands to heaven, thanking and praising God. She would then lay her hands on the person's head, and that one would fall to the floor! Not all of them would, but just those God willed to touch in this manner. But I would say that our Heavenly Father gave this love tap to the majority of these people. Also, I must mention that in many instances, she did not lay hands at all, but as God willed, they too were slain gloriously. Yes, the majority was given this love tap by our Father God. Well, now that was just too much! What a sham! Who were they trying to fool? I was in fact calling them a bunch of fakes and this whole scenario a grand travesty. I just did not believe it. She was a fake, and the people were fakes, phonies, etc. Oooh, I was going to pay gloriously for that kind of thinking. Imagine questioning God's sovereignty! The service was soon over and all began to depart. Those healed were joyfully praising God in awe and wonder as they exited, and probably still are to this day; those not healed no doubt were wondering why. And the rest were thankfully praising God in their hearts for the healing and power of God they had just witnessed. Somehow, some way, hopefully they fully determined in their hearts to make an effort to witness to those persons they felt through the leading of the Holy Spirit were in need of salvation and to disciple them along the way.

Several weeks passed by as I unsuccessfully tried to dismiss from my mind the fantastic Kathryn Kuhlman service, but to no avail. It all kept going over and over in my mind with no let up. The Holy Spirit was now determined to bring me into the Kingdom, and as you will see, there was absolutely nothing I could do to stop this unfathomable glorious crown of salvation I was shortly to receive.

Several more weeks passed, and my dear friend (who was the cause of all this) called to tell me that Miss Kuhlman had a service every month in the Los Angeles Shrine Auditorium. (Her home base was in Pittsburgh, Pennsylvania.) Why did she call me? She didn't really believe in the divine supernatural evidenced by Miss Kuhlman's ministry, and now probably more so in that her son's vision was not restored. Regardless, Lois and I decided to make the trip; we were always open for something different to do; we loved the Arizona and California scenery, and this was an opportunity not to be passed up. The necessary arrangements were made along with a group of others who were also interested in Miss Kuhlman and her fantastic ministry. In fact, there were two busloads of us from Phoenix. This was great. I was going to kill two birds with one stone: first, to let the bus driver do the driving while I would get the benefit of the scenery; and second, to prove that Miss Kuhlman was a fraud one way or another. I was determined to scrutinize the whole service with harshly critical eyes.

Upon our arrival in Los Angeles, we had an early dinner, met with several other Christians in our group, sang a few songs in the seminary auditorium, and went off to bed. One thing I had been observing about these born again Christians was that they were united spiritually. Sunday morning we had breakfast and joined our bus group and were off to the Shrine Auditorium, arriving there about 10:00 a.m. The doors did not open until 1:00 p.m. When the doors finally opened, we literally poured into the auditorium. Lois and I, as well as the remainder of the two busloads from Phoenix, were given reserved seats about three-fourths of the way down—rather close to the stage. I imagine this courtesy was shown to us in that we had traveled some eighteen hours or so and were given preferential treatment. This is my own observation. By headcount, there were more than ten thousand of us, including some who had been there since 6:00 a.m.

Now let's backtrack here. We didn't know it at first, but before the trip was over, we realized that most of the people on the bus were already "born again" believers. They were different, and it showed. I heard those words for the first time in my life at the first Miss Kuhlman service several weeks previously in Phoenix. Intermittently, different people on the bus would go up to the front and give their "testimonies." It was all Greek to me. I didn't even know what "testimony" meant, and I wasn't too interested yet! Time slowly passed—we semi-dozed; we appreciatively viewed the scenery; we sang more songs. Lois and I began to wonder what on earth we were doing on this bus full of kooky people. Some were talking, some quietly singing, and some praying in "strange languages!" I remembered the expression (tongues) before—probably at that first meeting in Phoenix. We were a little nervous at times, and then again decided to enjoy it. After all, what could they do to us?

About halfway to Los Angeles, a wonderfully gentle man, undoubtedly a minister (but not necessarily), asked a question: "Does anyone want prayers for anything?" Well, in six to eight hours I must admit I was doing a lot of thinking and wondering what this was all about and what I was doing on that bus! Stubbornly, I recognized the fact that I certainly needed some kind of help. Since I had been taught to pray the Lord's Prayer from the time I was old enough to talk, prayer was nothing new to me; perhaps there was a moment of dismissing this unknown cry for help. But before I could, suddenly and without further delay, my right hand shot up into the air. Later I realized that it was the Holy Spirit relentlessly continuing His holy pursuit of saving my soul for all eternity! How I thank God for His great mercy shown to me. The minister of "good news" approached me and began a conversation with me. I don't remember it entirely, but his first question was, "Did I know Jesus Christ?" Somewhat haughtily I replied, "I am a Catholic." (I really never knew that that meant either.) He again said, "Do you know Jesus Christ in a *personal way?*" I had to admit that I did not. He gently asked me if I had been "born again," and truthfully I replied, "I don't know what you are talking about." He asked me several more questions in the most gentle and loving way, and finally he asked if I wanted eternal life in heaven. And, praise the Lord, I responded "yes." Then he asked me to repeat after him the following prayer: "Precious Jesus, I believe You are the Son of the Living God; that You came to earth as a little babe; that at the age of thirty-three years You were crucified for my sins and the sins of the whole world; that You died and rose again in three days; and that You are now seated at the right hand of Almighty God in heaven. Lord Jesus, *I am a sinner. I repent* of my sins and ask You to forgive me. Lord Jesus, come into my heart and be my personal Lord and Savior." Well, as I began to repeat the words just spoken, all the pent-up heartache, trauma, brokenness, sadness, sinfulness, hopelessness, and frustration broke loose. The stubborn self-will had broken, and I was sobbing my heart out in repentance until I thought it would surely break into pieces. All my miserable life drained out in that humbling confession of being a sinner and asking for forgiveness. What a beautiful, refreshing, cleansing took place in my heart. (I had just been re-created—I was a new creation in Christ—but of course I would know that as time passed.) Now my friend, Lois, also basically repeated just what I have outlined above; however, she didn't break up at all. We are all *unique;* perhaps she didn't have as much to be remorseful about as I had. However, she did have her heart broken in her early thirties when, just five days prior to getting married, her fiancée died of a sudden heart attack. Yes, she had anguish of heart and soul and never did marry. She too by "faith" accepted Jesus into her heart to be Lord of her life. She had been a believer, as I had, in Jesus, but she had not been "born again" until that Saturday, June 24, 1971, on that bus to Los Angeles. I had been *beautifully born again* at the precise moment I asked Jesus to forgive me of all my sins and to come into my heart and be Lord over my life. I publicly made *confession* with my mouth that I truly accepted Jesus Christ as the Son of God. Romans 10:9 states, "That if you confess with your mouth, 'Jesus is Lord,' and believe in your heart that God raised him from the dead, you will be saved. For it is with your *heart* that you believe and are *justified,* and it is with your *mouth* that you confess and are saved" (emphasis added). No pomp, no ritual, no ceremony—just simply, humbly, beautifully giving your life to Jesus. I was on a bus trip, going to a Christian meeting in Los Angeles, when God spoke to my heart. That, my dear reader, was the *most important decision* of my entire life. You, at this point, cannot totally understand it, but by faith you are willing to believe and get on with this walk into the Kingdom of God for all eternity.

Now let's get back to the service. The entire atmosphere was building up with intense anticipation of the unknown. During the praising and singing, hundreds of people in the audience were lifting both hands in the air (I tried, but they felt like two one-ton beams). I just could not lift them up (pride—here we go again). I have since heard a beautiful interpretation of lifting hands in the air: just as a child raises his arms to be raised up by the parent, so we too raise our arms in total loving surrender to our merciful Father. God is now my Father since I am born of His Spirit. We want Him to lift us up out of this life of utter chaos, dejection, rejection, poverty, misery, etc. We surrender to Him and His wisdom; we accept Him as little children. In Luke 18:17, Jesus spoke these words: "Suffer little children to come unto me, and forbid them not: for of such is the kingdom of God. Verily I say unto you, Whosoever shall not receive the kingdom of God as a little child shall in no wise enter therein" (kjv). (I now love to raise my arms to my Father to pick me up—and He does.) Jesus is telling us that we must come to Him in faith as little children, not as super-intellectuals. That takes a bit of humbling, doesn't it? Your great big ego gets in the way, doesn't it? *Pride,* the murderer of men, is indeed the strongest of adversaries. Are you going to let a murderer prevent you from having eternal life? That is what pride is, a murderer of men. Only you can make the life or death decision. C'mon, use your heart. Your head simply cannot give you everlasting life in God's presence, but your humble heart can. Can't you hear your heart? Just listen.

Miss Kuhlman was softly speaking, constantly praising the Lord with her head tilted back and gazing into the spiritual realm. She was radiant with the glory of the knowledge of God. There seemed to be a holy, hushed atmosphere of wonder and awe. Something was about to happen, and yes, she began by saying the Holy Spirit was healing someone of deafness. She motioned to a certain area in the auditorium. She continued, "Accept your healing; you are healed. Praise and give thanks to Almighty God." On and on and on she continued, naming and calling out one healing after another. Finally, she said, "All of you with back ailments of any nature, rise up and stand. God is going to do a mass healing of backs." Well, interestingly enough, I had been in a very serious accident sometime previously to that meeting, having had a vertebra crushed when I was thrown backward under the dashboard of the car on the way home after "doing the town." For ten days I had lain motionless with a swollen stomach about the size of a baby whale. This had to return to normal (I weight only about 100 pounds) before they could "cast me"—my eyes were the only things I was able to move. After the ten days had passed and I returned to normal, they proceeded to wrap me in the body cast. I remained hospitalized for, I think, five or six weeks. I was in that body cast from my neck to below my hips for three months, and after being cut out of it, I was confined in and out of one of those horrible stave girdle garments. I was out of commission for almost one year before returning to normal. At times, my back did ache when I was exceptionally tired, and I valiantly tried to bury the thought of calcium buildup around that particular vertebra—but in a sense there was a silent, certain dread of the unknown. Therefore, when Miss Kuhlman made the statement to stand up, after prodding from the two ladies on either side of me, I did just that. With that grain of mustard seed faith, I tried to understand and accept total healing of my back. Suddenly, inexplicably, my legs just gave way under me and I fell back into my seat. I tried to rise up again, but my legs were as flexible as cooked noodles, and again I fell into my seat. Literally, the starch had been taken out of me! I couldn't understand it, naturally. I was somewhat confounded and baffled—what was happening to me? Remember when I mentioned before that back in Phoenix I had called the whole thing a masterful fake? Ha, ha, ha, it happened to me! The *unexplainable*—the *supernatural!* Since I could not stand, I remained soundly seated in a somewhat dazed condition as if I were slowly going under anesthesia—just a wonderful, sleepy feeling of contentment. I loved it! Actually, I was under the power of the Holy Spirit.

Miss Kuhlman then asked those who had received healing of any kind to start approaching the stage to explain to her and the audience what had happened to them. I still couldn't budge. If I was healed, I didn't know of what; I was in a daze. Actually, in retrospect, I realize God had begun the process of the healing of my mind, my soul, and my memories, as well as giving me a special tap to my back. For your information,

I had previously been a total "mess"—and God knew exactly what surgery to perform. However, at this point, I believe it was the beginning of a progressive total healing of mind, body, and soul. The dear lady on my left had been nudging me to get up and go up and give my "testimony" of how God had healed me. She later explained how she also felt the power of the Holy Spirit and was amazed. Lois also felt the heat of the Holy Spirit and was perspiring profusely under her beautiful long auburn hair as she began to sense the majesty and glory of the Holy Spirit. Lois, my dear friend on my right, also was imploring me to get up. I didn't think I had been healed since I think I truly expected some sort of stabbing pain throughout my body, but actually I didn't know what to expect; nothing like this had ever happened to me before. And besides, I could not stand up on my noodle legs. My, oh my, I was in a beautiful euphoric state. I couldn't yet recognize the fact that something sublimely divine was taking place. Gee, it was great. I never felt this elated in my entire life. Talk about being on a "high."

During all the activity of the hundreds of people preparing to go forward, the ushers were joyfully corralling and leading them to the stage to be interviewed by Miss Kuhlman. It was my turn as the ushers finally helped me to the aisle. I immediately plopped to the floor; I still couldn't stand up. Mentally perhaps I was thinking that people came here to be healed, not to be incapacitated, which I certainly was at that time as the Holy Spirit was dealing with me. At this point, my knees were wobbling; my entire body was reacting in a sort of mild shaking palsy-type seizure. (I just don't know how else to describe it—I was quivering.) What on earth was wrong? Regardless, I loved every moment of it. The ushers raised me off the floor and had to totally support me as they carried me toward the stage—my dangling legs almost useless. On stage, one of the ushers left me propped up with the second usher. I was drunk under the power of the

Holy Spirit. (Of course I didn't know that until later.) En route to the stage, the ushers commented using words to the effect of "Wow, the Holy Spirit has lovingly zapped you in no uncertain terms." In the vernacular, I had a number done on me. The usher continued talking to me, and I began to regain a semblance of normalcy. Some of the starch was coming back into my legs and finally I could stand alone. After that, I saw several men trying to rise to their feet prematurely after being slain under the power of the Holy Spirit, and they literally were supported by men on either side as they staggered to their feet. I have seen many drunken men (I was once in the business), and that's what they looked like. However, they were under the power of the Holy Spirit—supernatural, and most difficult to explain.

Thus, again in explanation, I was under the power of the Holy Spirit. As yet, I had not been "slain"—that was soon to follow. And naturally I had no idea of what the usher meant when he said that the Holy Spirit certainly had touched me. Shortly thereafter, I was "slain" at the close of my interview with Ms. Kuhlman. Being "slain" means that God reveals His power in such a fashion that you fall utterly helpless to the floor! In the book of Acts, Chapter 9, Saul of Tarsus was on his way, seeking those believers in Jesus to take them back to Jerusalem (approximately 150 miles away) to be persecuted or perhaps put to death. Chapter 9, verse 3 begins: "As he neared Damascus on his journey, suddenly a light from heaven flashed around him. He fell to the ground and heard a voice say to him, 'Saul, Saul, why do you persecute me?' 'Who are you, Lord?' Saul asked. 'I am Jesus, whom you are persecuting,' he replied. 'Now get up and go into the city, and you will be told what you must do'" (Acts 9:3–6). Not only did Saul fall to the ground, but also he was blind for three days. Get your Bible out and read the rest. In like manner, remember I also took a long journey, eighteen hours or so, to California, to persecute Miss Kuhlman, and now you know the rest of the story!

My, how I love it when God manifests His power. Great Glory. Finally, it was now my turn to approach Miss Kuhlman to be interrogated as to what happened to me. Of course I was still in a daze; there could have been a million people out there, and it didn't faze me one bit. (Ordinarily I would have shrunk in terror to just stand before that many people, let alone carry on a sane conversation.) As she began questioning me, I felt I was responding in a perfectly normal manner except for the fact that I was in this intoxicating state of euphoria. She asked me what I had been healed of. I replied, "My back." She asked me to bend and touch my toes, and then to lean this way, forward, sideways, backward, etc. She then asked me to remove my high heels and walk back and forth. I did. I truly don't remember what else she asked me. She then addressed the audience after she was convinced that "something" had happened to me. She could tell just by looking at my baffled countenance, and she said, "I believe God has truly touched this body." Just as she was uttering that statement, I found myself draped on the floor. Oh, glory! God is so wonderful! It was getting better and better. I had been "slain" in the Spirit—that is the expression known to all believers. Now I knew what was happening to all the others before me: they were being "slain" in the Spirit by Almighty God. No one touched me! God did it, and I give Him all the glory. Hundreds of others before me had experienced the same phenomenon after they had given their testimonies. They were falling like dominoes, whether Miss Kuhlman was addressing them or not. God was sovereign and in total charge of the supernatural healing that Sunday afternoon, July 25, 1971. I can't explain it—I just know God did it. Somehow you are given the knowledge to *know* God did it. It's really nothing, and yet it's everything. It is similar to fainting, perhaps, but since I have never fainted in my life, that may not be the best description either. If passing out is wonderful, this might be something like that. How can we describe the supernatural? We cannot—it's supernatural. In the meantime, there was a mob of us stretched out on that stage floor. All were dead drunk, having been slain by Almighty God. He just gave us a wee experience of His omnipotent power at that time to let us know emphatically that *He is God and is in command.* God does have a divine sense of humor—wouldn't you agree? We literally were drunk with the Holy Spirit. It does *humble* you when you have the "rug pulled out from under your feet," so to speak. You revel in the experience; you are thrilled that God is God and now you emphatically know it; you are overwhelmed with love at His power; you are in reverent awe of Him.

After an undetermined period of time (after all, I was out cold), I slowly sat up and rose shakily to my feet. I was enthralled at God's omnipotence. I was humbled. Suddenly, as a flash, it dawned on me: I had been losing my hair and was terrified of going bald; after all, a good head of hair is a woman's crown of glory. All the anguish I had suffered was taking its toll in other areas of my body and not just necessarily my back, mind, soul, or spirit; the traumatic experiences and deeply embedded scars of my life were all manifesting within my body. I vividly remember it was *imperative* that I get back to Miss Kuhlman and ask her to pray for me. I was still in this euphoric frame of mind and slowly made my way over to where she was standing. I wrapped my arms around her neck and begged her to pray for me. Now, Miss Kuhlman, in addition to countless other feminine attributes, had a glorious head of wavy auburn hair. I sensed her deep compassion for me. (I wore a wig quite frequently and was "wigged" at this meeting.[1]) She had her crown of glory while mine was rapidly disappearing. She gently disengaged my arms from around her neck while fully gazing into my eyes and withdrew several feet from me. She then raised her eyes and arms toward heaven, and with that radiant upturned face, she said, "Lord Jesus"—and with that, I was gone again. I was flattened on the floor. God again most emphatically did show me that *He is God.* Remember how I ridiculed that first service I attended in Phoenix and how I refused to believe what I saw? God sovereignly proved to me that it was true. There I was again the second time on the floor, flat as a pancake, and again I do not know for how long a period of time. I do know, however, that when I regained my senses, I began to experience humbleness within myself and was in reverential awe of my Father. This emotion then became one of praise as I talked with God and told Him I always knew He could do anything and how happy I was that He revealed His power to me in this way. Oh, reader, I was full of joy, lightness, and glory. Wow—this is something else. It's no wonder that I literally floated back over to where my slippers were. I sat down on the floor to put them on. In this still beautiful euphoric state, I glanced over to the center of the stage where people were still "testifying" of their healing. They thanked God, praised Him, and whammo, they were "slain in the Spirit" and flattened to the floor. They just received a little love tap from our Omnipotent Father. Praise the Lord for His power. At that point, I glanced over at Miss Kuhlman and looked into her eyes. (I was perhaps eight to ten feet away from her). My eyes were drawn heavenward to the top of the auditorium. Everything and everyone were in a state of suspension; I didn't hear a thing, nor did I see anything except where Miss Kuhlamn's eyes were; my eyes were drawn heavenward. Then it happened—incredibly, two streams of fire were blazing down on me (perhaps like a laser beam). It seemed I was instantly reduced in size physically to about one-inch high—a peanut—an incredible sensation. I felt as if I were a tiny bug on the floor of the universe. Eyes of fire were gazing into my eyes. Revelation 1:14 describes the eyes of God the same way: "His head and hair were white like wool, as white as snow, and *his eyes were like blazing fire*" (emphasis added). That fire was penetrating to the very depths of my soul. Radically, I have never been the same since that time. I knew at that moment that God knew all there was to know about me; my entire life was nakedly exposed and my soul was bared before those penetrating, all-knowing eyes of fire. I knew then that I could never escape His watchful eyes. No one can; He knows everything about everyone, including you! And in glorious revelation I knew absolutely that God loved me with an infinite love, a love beyond description, a divine and holy love, a tender and compassionate love.

God had given me an in-depth look into the supernatural. I was given absolute knowledge that God is the Great Creator. God imparts instant wisdom at the precise moment it is needed. Needless to say, that lovely twilight zone lasted for hours; however, the dramatic intensity of the euphoric state was slowly diminishing as the hours passed by, but my spiritual understanding from that moment on kept increasing on up to the present. Let me say that when God decides to deal with a person who is seeking, He really does, so be prepared for anything gloriously divine to happen to you if you wisely decide to seek an audience with our Heavenly Father.

On the return trip to Phoenix, the passengers on the bus were urging me to go to the front and give my "testimony." Now I knew the meaning of that word. However, by that time, I began returning to my normal timidity versus the euphoric boldness exhibited before more than ten thousand people. Of course, as I explained previously, I was simply not fully aware of what a supernatural event was taking place within my life. Nonetheless, reluctantly, I did go forward to try to explain what had happened. Several of the people admitted that I had a look of bafflement and utter surprise when I was gloriously slain. Again, that is simply the understatement of the year. I have taken the liberty at this point to get out the dictionary to check on the word "surprise." This is what Random House has to say: "1. To come upon suddenly and unexpectedly; 2. To strike with a sudden feeling of wonder that arrests the thoughts; as at something unexpected or extraordinary; 3. State or feeling of being surprised as by something unexpected; 4. To come upon unawares or without visible preparation; 5. To catch unprepared; 6. To amaze, astonish; 7. Astound, to strike with wonder because of unexpectedness, strangeness, unusualness; 8. Amaze, to astonish so greatly as to disconcert or bewilder." And with the above, I simply rest my case.

Upon my arrival back in Phoenix, as I was walking down the street, I seemed to be walking with the sensation of "slow motion" and felt as though I was greatly bouncing twenty feet high in the air. Oh my, that too was an elevating sensation. This brings to mind when you are watching football on TV and they show a replay—it's always done in slow motion. That perfectly describes the way I felt when walking. Now I have a vague idea what drugs called "elevators" do to a user, but he invariably lands with a crashing thud as he comes out of it. Who needs drugs? You see, my "dead" spirit was now gloriously alive! It was literally leaping for joy. I, who had been dead spiritually for fifty-one years, had been gloriously regenerated—spiritually born again! I had that same sensation several times later and wondered if anyone could see my revived spirit bouncing and leaping for joy. I was delirious with unspeakable joy. I was giddy as a child anticipating Santa Claus, presents under the tree, the whole bit. I had been beautifully born again. Ah, blithe spirit!

Several months later, I flew to Los Angeles alone just to be part of the worshippers at the miraculous Kathryn Kuhlman service, to witness God's great and glorious majesty, and to worship and praise Him (along with the thousands of others) for who and what He is and for the way His is manifesting Himself to man. I was now a love slave of Jesus, corralled and branded forever by the Holy Spirit. I continually thank God for His Son, my Savior and Lord, Jesus Christ.

On the Monday following the first visit to Los Angeles, I literally bounced around the office. My co-workers knew something dramatic had happened to me. I was still much elated and was just coming down from a "very high trip." Briefly I tried to explain what had happened. It was beautiful in that they were very open, and in fact, several were seeking God in their own way as well. So the testimony of my experiences was received with joy and gladness, and I hope it gave them further stimulus to continue their search for Truth and the new birth.

Perhaps some words of explanation would be appropriate here with regard to the Charismatic. That's what I began to call myself after the new birth. Actually, we were the "come latelies" in the true Christian world. That big revival began somewhere in the 1960s with quite a flurry. Most denominations suddenly found members of their flocks being caught up in the renewal because of the dynamic experiences of healing, etc., happening to the most unlikely candidates. They wanted even more that they had from their local churches and were being catapulted into a high dimension. The majority of the Protestant denominations had taught their young all about Jesus from the time they could toddle. It was vividly apparent to me that they had a much deeper understanding of the scriptures than I had as a Catholic. (After all, I never attended any church living that far back in the backwoods, and I had no auto to get to the nearest town. That is why I had to be farmed out to continue my high school education. The wonderful families I boarded with were Christian and saw to it that I attended church every Sunday. I am very grateful for that.) Unequivocally, most Catholics worldwide were obviously more fortunate than I in their early training and have a far better understanding than I had. It is my understanding that an extremely large majority of Protestants claims to be "born again." The rest are regularly taught about regeneration and baptism by total immersion for the remission of sins and the infilling or baptism of the Holy Spirit for power to live a truly Christian life in whatever circumstances they might find themselves. So along the way and as the Holy Spirit now begins to get involved in our lives, we become somewhat inquisitive of these strange things happening around us and of which we are totally ignorant. God has to work very profoundly in the come latelies. I was fifty-one years of age, plunging blindly into the jaws of hell. God had to deal with me in an entirely different way than He does with good old Bible-toting Christians.

Eventually I slowly began to come down to earth with pondering and much awe. I tried to get back into my regular work routine, and of course I did, but with much élan and gusto; I wanted to please my Father by being the best secretary possible. Approximately ten days to two weeks after the return home, another subtle but exciting phenomenon began to surface. How much more is there? (It really never ends.) I discovered that I was avidly interested in the Bible. Now remember, before this experience, I was exactly like some of you reading this book—you couldn't get me to touch a Bible, let alone read it. Heavens, it was all Greek to me. But not any more! Praise the Lord! Inexplicably—yes, inexplicably—I found myself irresistibly drawn, like a magnet to metal, to read the Bible. Readers, my first Bible has been literally devoured. (I now have at least five in my possession.) Yes, I became divinely enamored of God's Holy Word with great intensity, curiosity, and reverence. I read and studied it morning and evening (at college, at noon during my lunch hour), every day without fail—two, three, or four hours every night. Plus I prayed every night perhaps from one-half hour to sometimes two to three hours in total thanksgiving for my salvation. Now, dear readers, in all my fifty-one years, no one, but no one, could get me the least bit interested in the Bible. Are you getting the picture? *No one can lure you in any way* to read the Bible except God's Holy Spirit. Again, I am referring only to those of us who never had the Bible training as children. Therefore, since I had been *dead* spiritually for fifty-one years, I had to be fed *spiritually* or remain a stunted spiritual babe. The Holy Spirit gently but firmly enticed me to study God's Holy Word—and how I reveled in that Holy Word. I couldn't stop reading it if I wanted to. The more I read, the more the desire grew to know more. God's hand was upon me and remains upon me to this day. No Christian was prodding me since Lois was the only Christian friend I had, and she wasn't near to encourage or inspire me to study. *No one in this world asked me to read that book.* Up to the time I was born again, I was doing my thing—saloon hopping, movies, nightclubs, sensual dancing, smoking, drinking, and men. Also, miraculously I discovered I was instantaneously healed of smoking, and I hated the word "liquor." In several days, I discovered I was healed of nail biting, a habit I had for most of my life; and as for men—well, I was definitely "cured" of them also. In fact, ultimately I developed a "brotherly" attitude toward all men, and it was good. I was naturally astounded and elated by these obvious healings, because that is what they were. In the natural, and as you all undoubtedly know, it is difficult to break anyone of those habits unless you are stranded on an uninhabited island with no cigarettes, liquor, or men or women. Please don't get the wrong idea about my being "cured" of men. I think they are just great, and God knew what He was doing when He created male and female. However, I already had two husbands, both very much alive and well. Naturally, God and only God could heal me of my desire for a husband; otherwise, I just wouldn't be able to handle that area of my life. Each person's life and experiences are different; God deals with us as individuals. I know profoundly to the very marrow of my bones that I am free to *not* break any of God's Commandments. It's very simple and very, very clear that I simply have no desire to take that major step again, even if I were able to. I now belong totally to Jesus, my spiritual husband. I am still very human, and at times I would appreciate some type of wholesome companionship with a male, but I believe that would be a temptation in itself, and so I simply pick up the Bible and lose myself in the glory of my life to be hereafter. Really, it's not difficult at all with the *power* I have in the Holy Spirit. That's one of the main purposes of being baptized in the Holy Spirit: to give us *power* to be overcomers, to win, and to be champions in the race we are now engaged in to the finish line. By now you should be getting some kind of a picture—are you? I believe you are! I simply *had* to read God's Word, just as an alcoholic has to have booze or a user has to have a fix. You simply become divinely addicted to the *Word*. It's so difficult to explain, but everything happened to me just exactly as I have described to this point.

My development in my understanding of God and what Jesus did for me and mankind is overwhelming me with love. I am in love with my Lord and Savior Jesus Christ. Further, I believe it is a common phenomenon in the Charismatic movement that the desire (avid desire) to study the Word is one of the positive indications that God has indeed touched your being and regenerated your once dead spirit into a dynamic, living spirit. Because the Word of God is all about Jesus Christ, I began to know and love Him more each day; I can't praise Him and worship Him and love Him the way I deeply feel. It's beyond my comprehension. I didn't want anything at this point in my life but to know intimately my Heavenly Father, His Glorious Son, and the Holy Spirit. I prayed constantly, I never went out socially, and I studied the Bible diligently—and was intrigued by the Old Testament as well as the New. You may have read the following statement: "The Old Testament is the New concealed, and the New Testament is the Old revealed." My understanding of the message just grew and grew and grew. God does impart supernatural understanding to the believer, as he needs. The more the believer studies the Word, the more God reveals supernaturally to the believer. There is a divine principle that states, "Those who have grown in grace and knowledge of Him are the very ones to whom He reveals still more. It isn't feasible to crash suddenly into the totally unfamiliar." (To the author of these words, they are so applicable to my own experience that I couldn't think of anything to equal them, so I just "borrowed" them to shed more light on the subject to help the dear readers of this book. Thank you, whoever and wherever you are!)

Now, just as there are mountaintop experiences, so there are also valley experiences. As you know, when Jesus was baptized in the River Jordan by John the Baptist, He was filled with the Holy Spirit and was led into the wilderness by the Holy Spirit. Luke 4:1–13 states:

> Jesus, full of the Holy Spirit, returned from the Jordan and was led by the Spirit in the desert, where for forty days he was tempted by the devil. He ate nothing during those days, and at the end of them he was hungry. The devil said to him, "If you are the Son of God, tell this stone to become bread." Jesus answered, "It is written: 'Man does not live on bread alone.'" The devil led him up to a high place and showed him in an instant all the kingdoms of the world. And he said to him, "I will give you all their authority and splendor, for it has been given to me, and I can give it to anyone I want to. So if you worship me, it will all be yours." Jesus answered, "It is written: 'Worship the Lord your God and serve him only.'" The devil led him to Jerusalem and had him stand on the highest point of the temple. "If you are the Son

of God," he said, "throw yourself down from here. For it is written: 'He will command his angels concerning you to guard you carefully; they will lift you up in their hands, so that you will not strike your foot against a stone.'" Jesus answered, "It says: 'Do not put the Lord your God to the test.'" When the devil had finished all this tempting, he left him until an opportune time.

Now, my dear friend, if Jesus, the Son of God, was tempted and tormented by Satan, so too will that person who is baptized of the Holy Spirit be tested and tempted. Personally, I feel that the more of a potential threat you are to Satan, the greater the testing you will undergo. Or, perhaps, the more corrupt you have been, the more he refuses to relinquish his hold on you. After all, until you are born again, you belong to his community of henchmen, indirectly and without your even being aware of it. You were a party to the corruption he deceitfully floods upon an unsuspecting humanity.

So, too, I had my first frightening experience several days after my return from Los Angeles. I had gone to work as usual, returned from work, had my dinner, and began my study of the Word and later prepared for bed. I was living alone, and at that stage (a newborn babe) I did not realize just how extremely vulnerable I was to satanic attack; I had just been initiated into the Kingdom of God and discovered I had much to learn about the tactics of and protection from the devil. I began to fall asleep. Suddenly I felt as though I were being pulled into a black, dark pit. That was all. But it was a terrifying pit. Of course, I immediately opened my eyes. The moment I closed them, it would happen again. Perhaps it was 11:00 p.m. when I retired. I wasn't too tired or sleepy so I kept opening my eyes—keeping them open as long as I could. Because I couldn't keep them open very long, I would close them momentarily. Instantly, I would be pulled into that black hole, the pit of hell, so to speak. I believe the last time I noted the clock, it was about 3:00 a.m. I didn't see how I could stand any more when mercifully God finally allowed me to fall into a deep sleep.

The next day I was off to work as usual. I thought briefly about the incident as imaginary and dispelled it. However, the second night, the same thing happened. Again, I was terrorized and could only pray to God to help me make it through the night. The third night, the same thing happened again. You see, if it were only a one-night episode, I could have explained it away as my imagination. But three consecutive nights in a row—that was something else. Naturally, I had all the lights on in the house. The next day I made several frantic telephone calls and finally located a "completed Jewess"—a Jewish woman who had accepted Christ Jesus as her Messiah. She and her Christian husband came to my home that evening. They counseled me, prayed with me, and taught me how to "protect" myself from the enemy, the devil, who hated me because I now belonged to Jesus, whereas previously I belonged to him. Oh, believe me, friend—it's all so very true. Satan cannot stand to lose a single soul. He wants to take you to hell with him. When he cannot succeed in enticing you back into the old sin life, he will harass you with every trick he can dream up to torment you. Thankfully, this couple provided me with necessary ammunition to reject the enemy as follows: "Satan, I resist you in the name of Jesus, and I command you to get out of here and let me alone, for it is written, 'Greater is He who is within me than you who are in the world'" (see 1 John 4:4). That is all there is to it. Satan knows when you don't truly have enough faith to believe the words you speak. That is why you must believe the Word; study the Word daily so that your faith will become strong. Romans Chapter 10, verse 17 says, "Consequently, *faith comes from hearing the message, and the message is heard through the word of Christ*" (emphasis added). Whenever you use the name of Jesus, as your faith gets stronger and stronger, Satan has to obey because Jesus defeated Satan at the Cross through His death and glorious resurrection. Satan has been defeated, but he goes around like a roaring lion and tries to intimidate the new believer who as yet doesn't know how to protect himself. But always remember that Satan is all bluff—he is defeated, and he is a lion without teeth. However, if you don't know that, and if you are not fully convinced in your faith, Satan will try to torment you through bluff because he knows your lack of faith. So it is imperative that you build up your faith as quickly as possible.

As a child, I had been bitten on the face by a dog on a leash as I leaned down to pet it. Ever since that time, my uncanny radar would spot a dog two blocks away. Immediately I would run onto any porch accessible and would climb into any unlocked automobile to avoid a confrontation with that dog. Mother would say, "Don't be afraid—the dog senses your fear and will become bolder and try to attack you. Put on a front; don't be afraid." But the dog always could sense my fear even though I tried to put on a brave front, and he would nip at my heels or try to jump on me. He knew I was afraid. So it is with Satan when you are a baby Christian. Satan knows that—so my only advice is that you had better grow up to maturity as quickly as possible and memorize 1 John 4:4 as quoted above. Since that was my first memorized scripture, it is deeply embedded in my very being—I quote it whenever necessary.

After my counseling from the Christian couple, I prepared for bed with renewed faith. As I began to fall asleep, I immediately began to sense the terror of the black pit. I quickly used the words outlined above—the Sword of the Spirit—and with aggressive authority began my attack against the enemy! He took off like a scared rabbit! It works! Now, of course, it won't work if you are not a child of God with the Holy Spirit indwelling you. How I constantly praise the powerful name of Jesus. That was my very first spiritual testing of the unseen foe, and victory was mine as I routed the enemy in the name of Jesus.

Evidently I had sufficiently passed the first test and was rewarded with several uneventful months—a short vacation before the next assignment.

The uneventful weeks had passed swiftly, and I began to experience a strange compulsion to come back East to my birthplace, Pennsylvania. My mother was then seventy-six years of age, and I felt deeply about her and wanted to get reacquainted with her. After several phone calls, she tried to convince me that now was not the time to come home. I had an excellent position at the Capital whereas the employment situation in Pennsylvania was tight; I would have difficulty finding a comparable position, so she said to stay there! But the Holy Spirit had something for me in Pennsylvania; I resigned and came home just before "Hurricane Agnes" hit the East Coast in June of 1972. Since God was responsible for the move back East, God also had a job waiting for me after a much-needed six-month vacation. It was a time for reflecting, meditating on the Word, getting reacquainted with my mother, loving her more with each passing day, and sharing with her how Jesus was now my life. During this six-month period, I did seek employment but not too enthusiastically. I was enjoying this first vacation since I left home at the age of fourteen or fifteen—fifty years of struggling with no let up. God engineered this vacation for me and was in the process of engineering and getting wheels in motion for my next position at the college.

During the six-month period before finding employment, I lived with my sister and her husband. They lived in a tiny town of less than one thousand people. They were both great nature lovers and would spend hours driving around the hills of Pennsylvania drinking in the delights and breathtaking beauty of that area. Her husband took advantage of the fishing season and the hunting seasons for deer, turkey, bear, etc. He expressed how grateful he was for the bounty of the county, naming it God's Country. He had eyes to see.

My sister was a registered nurse at a nearby community hospital and had the three-to-eleven shift for the previous twenty years in the obstetrics ward. Her schedule left me alone with her husband five nights a week. That presented me with ample opportunity, thoughtfully planned with the help of the Holy Spirit, to discuss the plan of salvation and my new birth. Evidently, the Holy Spirit had been preparing his heart to receive the Word. He was very polite, he questioned, and we had a rewarding time together discussing our Savior. He was most receptive. After an hour or so of conversation on various subjects, he would leave the house—he had places to go and things to do. I had to study my Bible, have contemplation time and prayer time, and then go to bed. I would go to my room at 9:00 p.m. every night, close the door, and begin my fellowship time with God.

During this time frame that God had allotted to me, and with the guiding help of the Holy Spirit, I gently but firmly tried to explain all that had been happening to me since July 24, 1971, on that bus to California, when I was born again. In the beginning, they thought I had flipped my lid; however, little by little they decided that since I was one of the family, they would tolerate and humor my unorthodox condition. At one time, during an intimate conversation with my sister, she revealed to me that her husband had suffered two heart attacks in previous years—one was considered a mild warning, but the second was a definite danger signal. She was naturally most concerned and was diligent in closely monitoring his activities as well as his medications. When he had his third attack, I visited him at the hospital, and quite naturally the conversation led to Jesus. He was very willing and accepted Jesus into his heart. Perhaps he sensed he didn't have much time left—another attack and he would be gone. We prayed together with my leading him in the sinner's prayer, and he asked Jesus to come into his heart. Jesus did. A short time later, my brother-in-law had his final heart attack and was gone before the ambulance arrived to get him to the hospital. Do you believe the Holy Spirit was prompting me to return home for a reason? I do—one of the first reasons was to lead my brother-in-law to the Lord, and how I praise God that I obeyed the Holy Spirit. God had much work for me, and that was just the beginning. We never can see the end result at the beginning of some of the events taking place in our lives, but afterward we realize that God was at work.

Another assignment arose quite soon involving my half-sister, who lived in Chicago all but the first fourteen years of her life. She finally retired at sixty-five, having worked all those years in Chicago. Her husband preceded her in death in 1964. I believe that was the same year our father died. After several years of retirement, inexplicably she felt compelled to come east for some unknown reason. She really didn't want to make that move. My mother was her stepmother, and while there was never really the deep maternal love of a mother-daughter relationship, there was love and respect. I believe that she, too, just as I, wanted to renew her acquaintance with my mother, visit our birthplace, look up whatever childhood friends were still in the area, and just enjoy the final years of her life. She lived life to the fullest to occupy the void the situation had tragically presented, and she met the challenge with courage and bravery. Finally, she sold her home, got her affairs in order, and came to Pennsylvania.

One day as I stopped by to visit with her, she was watching the movie *The Robe.* (Joy, joy, joy—opportunity was knocking. Hallelujah!) She mentioned she enjoyed religious movies occasionally. That was just the door the Holy Spirit had opened. We began to talk about the Lord, and I began to explain how God was working in my life. I gave her a brief sketch of that bus trip to California, and needless to say, she was most intrigued. Upon my departure, I'm certain the Holy Spirit prompted me to suggest that she might begin to study the Bible, beginning with the Gospel of John. To me, it is so beautiful in revealing the truth, beauty, gentleness, and nature of our Lord in a manner that is easily understood by all who read it. The very soul of our Lord is laid open as He proclaims His relationship to His Heavenly Father and the purpose of the events that were to take place at the Cross. One cannot escape the fact of His total obedience to the Father, His humbleness, His divinity, and His great compassion for humanity for whom He obediently and willingly gave up His life.

Several weeks passed, and I again dropped in for a short visit. I again brought up the subject of the new birth and asked if she was ready to ask Jesus to be Lord of her life. Much to my delight, she stated she was eagerly anticipating this visit so I could lead her in the sinner's prayer. There you have it. She had been brought East by the gentle wooing of the Holy Spirit so I could witness Jesus to her and lead her in the sinner's prayer, and the angels rejoiced as she was led into the kingdom of believers. Prior to her regeneration, she shared that she really didn't know why she came East—she just felt that she had to for some strange reason. Now she knew the reason. Within a year's time, she felt the need to return to Chicago; she had an unsaved daughter and knew what she must do. Shortly thereafter, she discovered she had cancer, and it was only a matter of time that she went to be with her Lord in June of 1980. Coincidence? Hardly—God's ways are always perfect, and His timing is also perfect.

After my arrival from Phoenix, I moved in with my sister. Being only a year-old babe, so to speak (spiritually), I did make a lot of noise. I now know I came on too strongly; my sister thought I was slightly off balance (to put it politely), and I had to convince her otherwise. We have grown quite close, however, and she had given me quite a large sum of money, which I needed to purchase a home in Florida. After residing there for eight years, I finally sold the home and came back to Pennsylvania. I tried to repay the money she had "given" to me, but she flatly refused to take it. This year (1992) she again gave me a large sum of money to purchase another home even though we are at odds with each other now and then. No big thing; just sister spats. However, I know this is a testing time for me—the area of "patience." I love her for her understanding of my financial needs. She perhaps doesn't realize it, but of course, I see the hand of God in this situation, and I am looking forward to His further working in our lives.

Vacation time was over and I did find employment at a small college seventy miles away from my sister's and mother's hometown. Naturally, I did not hook up my TV set or play the radio for *five years!* Actually, I never did much of anything except study the Word, pray, and of course read good books written by others who had met the Lord Jesus. I attended endless prayer meetings—anything that had to do with glorifying God, you would find me there. I had been spiritually dead for fifty-one years, which was more than enough, and since I was now born again spiritually, I just couldn't learn fast enough to satisfy this *constant* never-ending hunger to know all about my Lord. I had an unquenchable thirst for more and more knowledge of the living God. Since I was now alive spiritually, my spirit had to be fed with daily spiritual food (the Word), spiritual vitamins, just as my body required to be fed three times a day.

It really isn't necessary for me to go into the details of how I was selected for the position at the college, but I did score the highest when taking the required state exams. There were three candidates in the final selection. I was the oldest and didn't think I had a chance, but I was selected and stayed on the job for nine and one-half years. God did it!

Before going on to the next exciting chapter, I would like to share with you the fact that the nine and one-half years of my college experience were extremely rewarding. The born again student members who were working part-time in the computer center and with whom I had daily contact were interesting, refreshing, and most rewarding. When you are a true believer, there simply is no dichotomy with regard to age, sex, race, color, creed, philosophies, material riches, or poverty. We are all one in Christ if we have made Him Lord of our lives. If you cannot accept this fact, you simply have not been regenerated.

See John Chapter 17 where Jesus prays for His disciples just prior to His crucifixion. Verses 20–23: "Neither pray I for these alone, but for them also which shall believe on me through their word; that they *all may be one;* as thou, Father, art in me, and I in thee, that they also may be one in us: that the world may believe that thou hast sent me. And the glory which thou gavest me *I have given them;* that they may *be one,* even as we are one: I in them, and thou in me, that they may be made perfect *in one;* and that the world may know that thou hast sent me, and hast loved them, as thou hast loved me" (emphasis added).

I think you will be deeply blessed by our Savior Himself if you, with an open heart, read the entire chapter. God bless you.

Chapter 3

The French Revelation

During my first few weeks at the college, I met a precious Catholic employee who had been born in France and who worked in the dame department as I.[2] Needless to say, I found a most receptive listener who let me "tell all" about meeting Jesus and the spiritual experiences I have written about. Surely the Holy Spirit had prepared her heart! Wonder of wonders, she believed everything I revealed to her. She, too, worshipped our Almighty God and was aware of His omniscience, omnipotence, and omnipresence! We became fast friends. One reason for the friendship was that she was from the Old Country (France) and my parents were also from the Old Country (Poland), and since we both had Catholic backgrounds, we had a natural common denominator. Our domain at work was the computer center—she in the technical area and I in the administrative. Invariably, we took our coffee breaks at the same time and went out to lunch quite frequently, which we both enjoyed very much. She became a very dear friend to me, and I love her in Christian love.

One day I became aware that I hadn't received any calls from her (I'll call her Michelle) to go on coffee break or lunch. Inasmuch as we were all so busy, I didn't make a criminal case of the situation. However, after several weeks had gone by, I began to sense that I may have offended her in some way—perhaps she was tired of hearing all about my love of Jesus and just decided that "enough is enough." I again resigned myself to the situation and dug deeper into the Word to console myself.

After about three weeks of silence, Michelle called and asked if I would care to go to lunch with her. She had something to tell me. Naturally, I was delighted. However, she cautioned me not to jump to any conclusions about what she had to share with me—not to make "something" out of it! My heart leaped for joy! I superbly restrained myself and decided to be "cool." I, of course, hadn't the vaguest idea of what she had to tell me. Who can fathom God and His fantastic modus operandi (M.O.)?

At lunch she shared with me the following dynamic revelation. She did not receive it in quite the same way I did— in fact, I did read very much in the revelation. She had been avoiding me because she was fearful I would make too much of what she believed to be just a dream. In her dream, she, her husband, and I were in France. We were in the Catholic church she had attended all her life until she left that country in her early twenties to come to America with her American husband. No one else was in the scene. The three of us were gazing upward at the Icon, a sacred Christian pictorial representation of Christ, which was located in the upper portion of the church structure toward the exit. Suddenly, as she continued to study the face of Jesus, His precious eyes began to gently flutter and then opened completely! Jesus gazed deeply and lovingly down at Michelle and said to her in French, "Listen to her [Jesus meant me]; everything she has revealed to you is as it should be!" That was all He said. Furthermore, she was instantly awakened after the dream and was truly alarmed and frightened because of the utter reality of it. It was so very, very real. Consequently, she had been avoiding me and needed time to dwell on the dream and what it meant.

What a confirmation Jesus had given me through Michelle of my testimony and witness of my born again experience. Isn't God fabulous? He had a dual purpose in that through Michelle's dream, God further advance my faith and my belief in sharing the Word. Needless to say, this gave me a much-needed boost that what I had been sharing with her was the truth. Secondly, perhaps it was to arouse Michelle to the fact she had to now move forward in her spiritual life. I simply accepted the dream/vision in its beautiful, simple, yet profound revelation. Since Michelle was French, Jesus spoke those words to her in her native French. Praise God—He uses everyone and every situation imaginable for His glory.

Michelle continued that when awakened from the dream, she felt great awe because it was so real, but she didn't want me to make something out of her dream. God was speaking to her so lovingly and beautifully. He reconfirmed my testimony about all that had been previously written to this moment. She, however, believed her final destiny was Heaven without the born again experience. I, being Catholic, wondered why I had never been convicted about being Heaven-bound until *after* my dynamic meeting with the Lord Jesus. In fact, I knew I was hell-bound without a doubt. As I recall, I gently explained to her how divinely blessed she was that God spoke to her personally in that dream, and in fact said to her, "Listen to her"—indicating that perhaps she, too, must seek something deeper in her life. After all, God sovereignly spoke to her (I've never had

God speak to me in a dream like that) to let her know that what I had been witnessing was true. God sovereignly gave her that divine revelation of Himself—He spoke to her directly in her native tongue. How marvelous in His ways is our God.

God had convinced me to completely bow out of the scene at that point and let the Holy Spirit do what further work was necessary in her life. I obeyed. Months went by, and nothing seemingly was happening.

One day in the mail I received an exciting brochure from the Full Gospel Businessmen's Fellowship International about a trip to the Virgin Islands. The brochure said to immediately respond if I was interested. Was I ever! It was to be only a seven- or eight-day cruise. We would fly out of Washington, D.C., to Puerto Rico, then board our ship, cruising at night and visiting some of the scheduled islands during the day. A super added bonus (to me) was a brief visit to Caracas, Venezuela, for a day. Naturally I mentioned the trip to Michelle—I asked if she was interested in going on the trip with a group of born again believers. She was! (The Holy Spirit had done His work.) We went. Originally, Martinique was one of the islands we were scheduled to visit, but it was withdrawn from the itinerary because of the minor political unrest at that time on the island. I believe Michelle wanted to make the trip primarily because it would give her the opportunity to speak her native tongue.

The hosts of the trip were the famous Jacobs Brothers singing team. Providentially we were seated at the same table with two of the Brothers and their wives for the entire trip. Talk about "divine planning." I couldn't have arranged that situation even if I wanted to. But God did!

Of course in due time, and I truly believe by the prompting of the Holy Spirit, it was inevitable that I began to share a few facts to one of the Brothers about Michelle and her glorious dream. Of course by now you already know the outcome. They had quite a session sharing the Word with her, and as I understand it, she reluctantly did say the "sinner's prayer" with the leading of the Jacobs Brothers. She strongly believed she was heaven-bound before being counseled. So the seed was planted, but to date I have not detected any dramatic change in her life. As I explained at the beginning of this work, some experiences are very subtle (but dynamic), and I believe this to be the situation with Michelle's dream/vision. Of course, God isn't through with her by any means, and I am excited about how He will manifest His glory in her future life.

Leaping forward now to 1988 (or thereabouts), I did have a conversation with Michelle, and she revealed to me the following. A Catholic born again Charismatic priest was paying an unprecedented visit to her church. She, her husband, and their two daughters, home from college, went to that evening service. Near a closing point of the service, the priest invited anyone who desired to receive a blessing to come forward. Michelle, her husband, and their two daughters dutifully went forward.

I'm laughing now as I recall Michelle saying to me earlier, "No one is going to push me to the floor." Of course, you again know what happened—she, her husband, and the two daughters were all slain in the Holy Spirit! Praise the Lord. One family now had received a love tap from the Holy Spirit. I'm certain the seed is now growing and will continue to grow as they continue in their lives.

In conclusion of "The French Revelation," I had previously made the statement that God never reveals to us any more than we can absorb at any given moment. Thus, with Michelle, God majestically opened the door of heaven to her through the dream and through the prayer of repentance as she was led by the Jacobs Brothers. Initially I had planted the seed, the Jacobs Brothers watered the seed, and the Holy Spirit will give the growth if she applies herself earnestly to studying the Word. It's entirely up to her just how she will mature spiritually. What will be the final outcome in Michelle's life? Only God knows for certain, and I believe it will be a continuing beautiful, spiritual development in accordance with God's will.

Chapter 4

Additional Unfolding of the Supernatural/ Spiritual

*A*fter our return from the Virgin Islands cruise, I once again settled down to my normal routine in the computer center. It was about that time that a new staff member was added to the administrative area. Since I was the only secretary in the department, it was inevitable that we would have to communicate with each other with regard to various and mundane topics such as learning the basic mechanics of the department. Once we became comfortable with each other, we began cautiously comparing notes, and in so doing, discovered we both knew "Jesus." He, too, had been initiated into the kingdom just a few short years before at that time, and from our sharing, he was concerned that perhaps he had made the wrong move in joining the college.

He was beginning to feel that perhaps he should have enrolled in a Christian seminary. He, too, had a dynamic encounter with the Lord while seeking the "new birth."

One day during coffee break, he asked me if I had received the baptism of the Holy Spirit. I had not, and did not understand. He explained it to me and referred me to Mark 1:8, which says, "I baptize you with water, but he will baptize you with the Holy Spirit." He also quoted Luke 3:16: "John answered them all, 'I baptize you with water. But one more powerful than I will come, the thongs of whose sandals I am not worthy to untie. He will baptize you with the Holy Spirit and with fire.' " One more scripture is found in John 1:33: "I would not have known him, except that the one who sent me to baptize with water told me, 'The man on whom you see the Spirit come down and remain is he who will baptize with the Holy Spirit.' " The same man—John the Baptist—spoke in all the above scriptures. Jesus Himself baptizes us with His Holy Spirit after we have been born again and properly prepare our hearts to ask Him to infill us with His Holy Spirit.

My new friend in Christ then informed me that there was going to be a Full Gospel Businessmen's meeting in Williamsport, Pennsylvania, and asked if I would care to go along. He spiced up the conversation by telling me that the "guest" speaker was to be a Catholic nun from Ann Arbor, Michigan. Well, that's all it took—naturally I just had to see and hear a real live Catholic who was on fire for the Lord. The meeting was great, with much praising and singing to the Lord. Several good testimonies were given, and then the main speaker herself started. She gave an excellent talk and explained in detail that she was not being spiritually fulfilled where she was teaching and decided to give up the profession of being a nun. She continued to explain that after much soul searching and praying to God for answers, she began to receive an understanding of how God wanted to use her. She went on and shared her born again experience and the baptism of the Holy Spirit. Furthermore, God was going to send her into all parts of the world to heal, to bridge the lack of understanding among all denominations, and to witness to the glory of God.

And so it was as God had revealed to her. She ultimately did go to many countries in Europe and spoke at hundreds of meetings in America. People of all denominations were flocking to hear the witness of this remarkable woman. This charming nun had received many gifts of charisma from the Holy Spirit, including speaking in a supernatural language. During the meeting, people were praying, singing, praising, prophesying in different languages as well as in English, and translating the "other languages" into English. God was using her as an ambassador of good will. But the primary purpose of such meetings is to lead non-believers into the born again experience and of course to bring glory to Jesus. All who wanted to be born again or to receive the baptism of the Holy Spirit could do so after the meeting was over. Prior to this meeting, I was really being "convicted"—a constant restless feeling of something still to be done. A large group was waiting to be baptized after the meeting but unfortunately, because of the lateness of the hour, we had to vacate the premises. The rest of us were to receive the baptism the next day at a Catholic church in a nearby town if we so desired. Of course, I desired!

Upon my arrival, the sisters were having a dinner in honor of the guest sister from Ann Arbor. As is customary, we had prayer, singing, praising, and worshipping God. After dinner, she and the president of the Full Gospel Businessmen's Fellowship of that area were going to counsel me for receiving the baptism of the Holy Spirit. Notice specifically that a Catholic nun and a Protestant minister were to assist me. Evidently it just had to be that way. Now, because of the unsuccessful attempted indoctrination

I had received regarding Cayce, yoga, reincarnation, astral projection, the Area for Research and Enlightenment, etc., everyone there was in deep prayer for God to lead us.[3] They instructed me to repeat after them that in the name of Jesus I was to renounce everything contrary to the teaching of the Bible. I vehemently denounced my belief and hatred of all evil—witchcraft, ouigi boards, reincarnation, Cayce, etc.—until they and I were absolutely positive I didn't have any hang-ups left within my mind. Then we prayed again. I can't remember exactly what words were used, but after I had been thoroughly cleansed by my denunciation of all those things that God abhors, I then asked Jesus to baptize me with the Holy Spirit. That was it. Nothing dramatic happened as during my born again experience. And I did not receive the gift of tongues as multitudes do. In a great many cases, the person who is seeking the baptism of the Holy Spirit receives the gift of speaking supernaturally to God immediately following his asking Jesus to baptize him. In my case, as I've stated, nothing happened. (Or so I thought at that time.) Again, in a vast majority of cases, the person does receive the gift of tongues as an indication that he indeed has been baptized of the Holy Spirit. But Jesus stated quite simply that all who ask shall receive the baptism. Would a father deny his child bread? Of course not. Would Jesus deny the baptism of His Holy Spirit? Of course not. Also, those who did not believe in God or Jesus, but later had been born again, usually are given that particular gift immediately to absolutely assure them that they had been baptized and that something wonderful and supernatural has happened.

I wondered what was wrong with me. I needed and wanted the Holy Spirit to fill my entire being, and I expected to receive the gift of "tongues" just as many others had. I needed extra power in praying; in resisting temptation; in living a good, clean life; in witnessing; and in just being able to go on living. But the main purpose is to empower us with the Holy Spirit to be able to preach the Gospel of Jesus Christ and to be witnesses of our relationship with the living God and to pass this spiritual knowledge on to non-believers, to win lost souls for Jesus. Just because you don't begin speaking in tongues immediately after you had prayed for the infilling of the Holy Spirit doesn't necessarily mean you have not received the Holy Spirit. Remember, God is supreme and does as He wills. There are many ideas given about speaking in other tongues; some people are unable to relinquish their dominating control over themselves and will not allow the Holy Spirit to speak through them. I had all kinds of crazy ideas about speaking in tongues. However, I have been told repeatedly that sooner or later the tongues may manifest while praying, studying the Bible, doing the dishes, running the carpet sweeper, repairing the auto, driving to work, etc. You are not forced into anything. Subsequently, as the Holy Spirit deals in your life and you submit your entire being to the Lord, and submit your ego and control of your tongue, undoubtedly you will begin to speak in another language. As for myself, I was older, actually fifty-four years old—it's tough for an old hardened person of the world to "give in totally" and let God take over. It would be much simpler and easier for a younger person. I have never had the fluency of speaking in tongues as a good majority of other believers have. The Holy Spirit imparts diverse gifts when He infills believers and gives the gifts He chooses. The diverse gifts are given in 1 Corinthians 12:6–11: "There are different kinds of working, but the same God works all of them in all men. Now to each one the manifestation of the Spirit is given for the common good. To one there is given through the Spirit the message of wisdom, to another the message of knowledge by means of the same Spirit, to another faith by the same Spirit, to another gifts of healing by that one Spirit, to another miraculous powers, to another prophecy, to another distinguishing between spirits, to another speaking in different kinds of tongues, and to still another the interpretation of tongues. All these are the work of one and the same Spirit, and he gives them to each one, just as he determines." (I pray about "discernment of spirits.")

Ironically, however, it was during an illness when I was hospitalized and seeking God for healing that the Holy Spirit spoke through me for the very first time. It was simply terrific. Since then I do pray in my language, but only as I feel prompted of the Holy Spirit. I cannot zoom in on any of the above definitions of "gifts" absolutely, but since I have had supernatural visions, I feel strongly about discerning of spirits. Generally speaking, however, our entire supernatural being is being enlightened in wisdom and knowledge such as we never had before insofar as "what's it all about" is concerned. Inexplicably, we have a deeper understanding of God and the universe and the role we have in God's plan for our individual lives. Now our priorities are being established in the proper manner in accordance with God's will. We are now empowered to obey the Ten Commandments and the one *great* commandment that our Lord gave to the apostles in John 13:34: "A new command I give you: Love one another. As I have loved you, so you must love one another." That is it. You can see that love can do no harm to anyone. That's what it's all about, isn't it?

Speaking of loving one another, I had been reading of a supernatural vision of our Lord in Port Arthur, Texas, in the fall of 1971. Naturally, I had to go and check it out. I flew to Texas, got a rental car, and drove to the lady's home where the vision was seen. Our Lord Jesus is very humble— remember he was born in a stable. As I concentrated, looking at the screen door, the face of our Lord was quite visible. I had my camera and took some shots, but I still can't quite understand what I saw. This particular snapshot reveals Jesus looking at a fig tree in the back yard (there actually is a fig tree there). Biblically, the fig tree represents Israel. In Luke 21:29–31, Jesus is teaching His disciples regarding signs of the end of the age: "He told them this parable: 'Look at the fig tree and all the trees. When they sprout leaves, you can see for yourselves and know that summer is near. Even so, when you see these things happening, you know that the kingdom of God is near.'" Israel is referenced as a fig tree, and we know that she became a nation in 1948—the fig tree blossoming, as it were. Events are unfolding so rapidly in that tiny nation that the media can hardly keep up with it, and all that is happening will be in total fulfillment of prophecy.

Time as we know it will soon cease, and Jesus will return during the battle of Armageddon to overthrow Satan and all his allies and to set up His kingdom here to rule the earth for one thousand years, the millennium from Mt. Zion. Since evidence of this old world's final destiny will take place in Jerusalem, let's all be prepared for the outcome. Israel is the "key" to the final outcome of history. It's factual and scriptural, and both the Old and New Testaments prophesy of its role in the end time. As I stood there pondering what I was seeing, the lady of the house brought out her album containing pictures of our Lord she had taken at various times as displayed on the screen door. Her pictures reflected numerous scenes of Jesus, beginning with the familiar manger scene and on to the crucifixion. I was deeply moved and touched by all I had seen and heard from her. She was definitely a child of the Lord.

As I finally departed out into that great big state of Texas, I pondered with awe the vision I had seen. Since I had a rental car, I decided to drive until I could make up my mind whether to fly back or to just keep on driving. As I headed toward Arizona, naturally I became hungry and stopped at a small restaurant along the highway. Upon entering, I discovered that a black family apparently owned and operated the restaurant. I ordered my sandwich and began to eat. Then, for some strange reason, I began to scrutinize the young girl who had waited on me. She was perhaps fourteen years of age. Suddenly, such compassion began to arise within me that I just didn't know what was the matter. I wanted to cry. But why? I don't know. I just felt all mushy, loving, and compassionate inside and wanted to hug the girl. I reached in my purse and took out a watch locket I cherished, and I could not conceive parting with it for anything. It was not that expensive, but it was an article of jewelry I coveted above all my other jewelry. Now don't misunderstand—I had only about three good pieces of jewelry, but much of it was costume jewelry as is the case with most women who work in the marketplace. Why did I take that locket on the trip? I always wore my wristwatch. But God knew why. I surely didn't want to give up that watch locket (it was one of a kind). But strangely, I found myself saying to her, "Hold out your hand." She did, and I placed the locket within her outstretched hand and gently closed her fingers over it. First, though, she said, "Now why do you want me to do that?" At this point I said, "Because I love you." *And I did!* Ah, readers, there is no joy that can exceed the joy of seeing a radiant expression on the face of someone who is totally surprised by something we do. She was absolutely delighted, and she scampered to the kitchen, evidently to show the members of her family what I had given to her. In all sincerity, that was one of the sweetest highlights of my entire life. I myself did not do it; I was gently prompted by the Holy Spirit to express my love. Loving is giving in any and every way. As I mentioned before, I didn't dream of parting with that particular piece of jewelry; I coveted it. I took it with me because I coveted it, but I didn't wear it. Was it God working within me that caused me to take it with me? You be the judge of that. Do you see what I am getting at? The joy I derived by that single act of love made me feel like an angel of heaven. I was somewhat ecstatic with joy; I love everyone in the whole world. I was never taught to hate or despise anyone because of race or religion or politics. I detest and despise the mean and despicable things people do to people, but I don't hate them. I just love them.

I am being obedient to Jesus. Jesus is Lord of my life, and the Holy Spirit strengthened that commandment within me to love—and love is giving: a smile, a tender touch, a simple gift of any sort, a single stemmed rose, etc. *Wow!* Can you possibly imagine what repercussions that single Holy Spirit act must have had in that tiny community of black people? It was as though God was saying to me, "Child of mine, in this small way, this small act of love, there will be one less black person in the world who will not despise 'one white' person quite as completely as before." I felt such compassion for the entire black race and the associated horror of the history of the black people perpetrated by the early colonizers of this country. I was deeply moved. Don't you see how pleased my Abba must have been with His spiritual child? Who can fathom God and His marvelous M.O.? No one can.

And so we backtrack to the point where I, in faith, had asked Jesus to baptize me with His Holy Spirit on that Saturday afternoon at a Catholic convent. The following morning, I went to church and spent the rest of the day catching as many religious programs as possible. I studied the Word and retired early. I went to work on Monday and performed the usual routine upon returning to my trailer after work. I was asking God within my heart to help me find the words to express what happened to me that Monday night. After eating supper, doing the dishes, studying the Bible, saying my prayers, and worshipping God in the only way I knew how, I went to bed. As I relaxed and gently settled down, I began to sense, as the wings of a fragile butterfly, a glorious divine sensation of supernatural waves of love encompassing my entire body cascading from my head to my toes. I was being enveloped as a cocoon. I was caught up in the web of Almighty God and exquisitely embraced in sublime, divine love. Oh, the fragrant holiness of this encompassing of God's divine love is indescribable. Mere words are beggarly and totally inadequate when trying to describe the spiritual. The supernatural, divine, exquisite waves of love continued pouring over my body. The Holy Spirit was embracing me in the most adoring manner imaginable. And I *knew beyond a shadow of a doubt* that I was loved by God. I *knew* I had received the infilling of the Holy Spirit. I knew I belonged to Jesus and I was alive—my spirit that had been dead from birth was now vitally alive forevermore—alive to the glory, the supernatural—alive to the knowledge of God. I was totally protected by God just as a baby is protected within its mother's womb. I was safe within the bosom of my Father, my Abba. I knew *Him.* Such glory, such exquisite rapture, cannot be measured, described fully, or imagined beyond this world. It was spiritual love. I virtually was drowning in the glory and ecstasy of God's love for me. And so I fell asleep in the arms of divine love.

The second night, Tuesday, the same thing happened except there was also an immense surging of spiritual power throbbing in my left hand from the elbow down to my fingers. My left middle finger had been smashed as a child by a window falling down on it. It was abnormally slender and rigidly stuck straight out because my mother had placed a flat piece of thin wood against the finger and wrapped it to heal the fracture and bleeding. The end result was a stiff finger. The surging power kept flowing back and forth in that finger, and I just knew I was going to have flexibility I never had before, and it has happened! It is still somewhat abnormal in appearance (more slender than the middle finger on my right hand), but let's say it is fifty percent more flexible than before. God is healing me in the manner best for me.

Also, prior to my born again experience and up until this Tuesday night, I had been experiencing intermittent flare-ups of extreme pain in my left hip; it could have been as a result of the flattened disc I suffered during my auto accident mentioned earlier. I was really having difficulty falling asleep many nights for quite some time because of the pain. Again, there was a supernatural, powerful surging of energy encompassing my left leg and hip. Praise God, it was completely healed and I have never experienced pain since that night. And again I experienced exactly the same encompassing warm waves of divine love cascading from my head to my toes. I would try to say how long this continued, but I haven't the vaguest idea. But this I do know: God, my Abba, was holding me in His arms and comforting me just as a child who has been hurt is held in his mother's arms. Love is many faceted—a child receives physical love, and I received God's spiritual love—divine love.

The third day, Wednesday, was the same schedule as outlined above. I prepared for bed, said my prayers, and into bed I went. This night the supernatural divine waves of energy were more pronounced on my face, and in fact, it was as though my lips were being sealed. Now there is an expression in the Bible: "You are sealed by the Holy Spirit forever." Could this have been that expression?

During this "sealing" of the Holy Spirit, I began to smell something like burning sulfur. Now, I have never smelled burning sulfur other than matches, but I knew what I smelled. It was stronger than burning wood—much more acrid. In the Bible it teaches us that the Holy Spirit comes to baptize is with flaming fire; the Holy Spirit literally burns up the old dross within us and begins to scour and clean us up since He now resides in our bodies. The sulfur odor was so powerful that I thought perhaps that God was going to reveal a scene of hell to me. But He didn't. It was just the Holy Spirit scrubbing and cleansing and purifying my soul, literally! After all, every believer is the temple of the living God, and He will not live in an unclean temple. I have been keenly aware that everything that happens to me is literal and not just imagination. Also, I believe it was that particular night that I became aware of three tiny tongues of fire placed just above the temple of my left eye. I have since come to the conclusion that it represents God the Father, God the Son, and God the Holy Spirit—the Most Blessed Trinity. This manifestation is with me to this day. It was more pronounced back then, and on occasion when I would go from one room to another after I had turned out the lights, the three tongues of fire would seem to project from my head out into space. What a phenomenon! What a Holy God! Would you not say that God wants me to be ever mindful of His presence? I must respond with an emphatic "yes." [4]

Since the three nights of being baptized with fire and love, God wanted to make certain I would never forget it—that's why this happened three nights in a row. This night was Wednesday, and in addition to what I have just described above, the following left me groggy. I began to experience an entirely different supernatural phenomenon. Here is where God revealed pure, undiluted Holy Spirit *power* to me. My body began to pulsate, increasing in intensity as trillions of atoms were sizzling and fizzing within and without my body. (Of course, we all know we are composed of atoms.) It is absolutely mind fracturing as I now am trying to recall in vivid detail this revelation of revelations. I guess it's something like this: all the power that the Holy Spirit represents is now within my body. [5] I felt all-powerful. These trillions of atoms surging and surging within my body were telling me I was capable of doing just about anything (in accordance with God's will), like raising a person from the dead! Think about that. Jesus said we could do anything He did and even greater things than He did! In John 14:12, Jesus is speaking: "I tell you the truth, anyone who has faith in me will do what I have been doing. He will do even greater things than these, because I am going to the Father." Readers, I need to say this—we are all potential Jesus people, and Jesus Himself said further in John 15:7: "If ye abide in me, and my words abide in you, ye shall ask what ye will, and it shall be done unto you" (kjv). Also see John 14:21, where Jesus said, "Whoever has my commands and obeys them, he is the one who loves me. He who loves me will be loved by my Father, and *I too will love him and show myself to him*" (emphasis added). Jesus was manifesting *Himself* to me because He lives within me. Jesus raised several people from the dead. Lazarus had been dead four days, and Jesus raised him from the dead. We have that power—God sovereignly manifested it to me as described above. We have that *power* if we only believe, but we also must *abide* in Jesus Christ. We can believe, and the majority of believers do, but we are utterly and totally a failure as to abiding in Jesus the way we should to manifest His power within us—consequently, we are totally helpless and powerless. However, the potential power is there, and always will be within us, to be released when we have the faith appropriate to this spiritual understanding. God, in His infinite love for me, chose to reveal the power it takes to raise a dead man (the power of the resurrection). That "expression" was revealed to me by a Christian lady who was helping me in the battles with Satan. He never gives up. She had sent me several tapes on how to further protect myself from the harassment of the devil, and she in turn related to me the satanic torment she went through for a year before she understood our power in the Holy Spirit and how to repel the enemy. Further, the devil was tormenting me because I belonged to Jesus. The devil hates me and will torment me at every opportunity until I have strengthened my belief to such a degree that I can easily ward off satanic attacks. She then told me to ask the Holy Spirit to reveal to me the *power of the resurrection!* Alleluia—praise the Lord.

Intuitively through the Holy Spirit I knew God had revealed to me the power of the resurrection without my even knowing what it was! So that was the power it takes to raise a dead person—and it has since dawned on me that *I was dead spiritually* before my born again experience. This experience, the power of the resurrection, was God manifesting to me that I, too, had been raised from the dead spiritually! Fantastic revelation. Readers, let me say that there is nothing in this old world that can compare to coming into the knowledge of our glorious and majestic God, the Creator of this universe and everything that is. *Wow!* I get so wrapped up in the knowledge God has revealed to me that I could easily come unglued! I am a simple person, and I simply cannot find words lofty enough to express the inexpressible. But I think you are catching on.

The next morning as I left for work, I gazed around the trailer court and felt I could toss a few trailers into the air just as a juggler tosses plates into the air. I'm talking about trailers—I truly felt I could lift several. My faith at that moment was so great that I truly wanted to try. However, a word of caution: we do not have this power to produce sensational feats that will attract attention. One has to know from the Holy Spirit just how to proceed at a given moment in doing God's work. Now, in summation, this is what we have within our bodies—the power to be used to glorify God. It is the same power that Jesus had. It is power to serve the Living God; it is power to glorify Jesus in our way of life, work, play, reading material, and TV; it is power to resist temptation, evil, cheating, lying, etc. But above all, it is the power to spread the Gospel of Jesus Christ and to be a witness to others. Perchance at some point in time we will be called upon by God to help someone involved in an accident, illness, or whatever the occasion may be. As we exhibit our faith to the best of our growth and spiritual development, God will honor our faith so that He can be glorified in the name of Jesus.

Absolutely fantastic. I was speechless before God for weeks after that revelation. All I could do was worship, adore, thank, and praise Him for His love manifested to me.

There have been other manifestations of the supernatural—you be the judge of this one as to whether it was of the enemy or not. Keep in your mind that God is present in my mind constantly—never abating, consciously and unconsciously. In my eagerness to know what other believers are experiencing, I began devouring books of other born again witnesses, evangelists, and preachers by the hundreds. They, to me, are as alive as the pastor at church on Sundays. It's all teaching, researching, and learning.

One day I had purchased a book, *Reach Up for a Miracle,* authored by Don Basham, a writer who had himself experienced many battles with the enemy. Believe me, if I had known the result of reading it, I wouldn't have touched it with a ten-foot pole! It truly captivated my complete attention, and at every free moment, I would continue reading. (Incidentally, during this insatiable time of reading Christian books, at times I would read three or four books at the same time.) I think you will agree I certainly was ravenously hungry to learn all I could as quickly as possible.

This one particular evening, I was eating supper and reading *Reach Up for a Miracle* at the same time. All of a sudden, I was struck as though a bolt of lightning had zapped me from the top of my head to the tips of my toes. I froze. It was quite a powerful jolt, and I was somewhat stunned. I didn't know what had happened to me, let alone what to do. I was quite fearful and afraid to move. Incidentally, it was a clear summer day and still very light outside when this happened. After sitting there, barely moving an eyelash for possibly fifteen minutes to one-half hour—with the food getting all cold—I finally found the courage to gingerly rise from the table. I then called a Christian lady who came to the rescue with two other believers. They, naturally, had the Sword of Truth with them—the Word of God, the Holy Bible. They proceeded to pray for me and exercised their spiritual authority to "deliver" me of anything demonic. My dear readers, let me say this: when you are born again, even if you had a thousand demons inside of you, when you ask Jesus to forgive you of your sins, you repent of them, and then ask Jesus to come into your heart and be the Lord over your life, He does miraculously come into your body spiritually. Anything that may possibly have been within you is, in my humble opinion, literally blasted out of you. No power inside or outside of a truly born again person has more power than Jesus, and when Jesus moves in, everything evil must move out! What a baffling experience— but I still don't know what to make of it. Since I was somewhat frightened, I had to assume the "bolt" was from the enemy. Satan couldn't stand to have me learn more about his hatred of born again Christians, and the book went into much detail about the enemy and how he attacks us. No wonder the devil was plain mad! He just can't stand for us to know the ugly truth about him. On the other hand, God never frightens us; He chastises, yes, but never instills fear as I have described. So that experience is a little more light shed on the spiritual world after being born again. Jesus takes up residence in our hearts, and whatever should not be there is simply blasted out. We are *new creations.* Praise God for the simplicity and beauty of the born again experience. As for the "bolt"—it was just another attack on me by the enemy—he simply can't stand it when you go "all out" for Jesus.

Can you possibly wonder why I worship and adore my Jesus, who saved this wretched soul and lovingly has allowed (for learning purposes) such manifestations of the supernatural, spiritual world? I unceasingly praise Him, worship Him, sing to Him as I play my autoharp for Him, and talk and walk with *Him*, and He is ever on my mind. With regard to the autoharp, I was self-taught and really didn't necessarily want to go "public"—Jesus was all the public I needed at that time.

Whenever I would have difficulty falling asleep, I would get up and play the harp and sing softly to Jesus. One night as I was softly playing, I began to detect a glorious fragrance emanating from the harp. Naturally, my face was resting on the harp, and that is where the fragrance was coming from. Such a lovely scent! I was so delighted and full of joy. Was my Lord acknowledging my frail effort to sing praises and make music to glorify Him? Could it be that He would do such an unexpected thing? Was I dreaming? No, I wasn't dreaming—it's so true. After I stopped playing, the fragrance stopped emanating from the harp. Oh, the joy our Father derives from His children who express their love for Him in whatever ways possible. I am rapidly learning that the more you seek God, the more He reveals the spiritual world to you. He loves us so very much and wants us to apply ourselves and learn all we can about Him. After all, we are now "naturally supernatural" and should become aware of the new spiritual dimension.

The next day was Thursday—and that night nothing happened.

On Friday, however, I decided to pay a visit to my mother. She lived about seventy miles away, and I needed to tell her all about the revelations that had been given to me on Monday, Tuesday, and Wednesday. Naturally, she had much difficulty with what I told her, but being the loving mother she was, she accepted my story. I had every intention of staying over the weekend and returning on Sunday. It just didn't turn out that way.

After having a long talk with my mother about how God was in charge of my life, it was time for lights out, and Mom lovingly tucked me into bed as though I were a little child. Spiritually, I was just a child. She loved me so very much. I said my prayers and was in a beautiful frame of mind, never giving a thought to anything happening (I never do!). But I was wrong again. Glory! I snuggled down into bed and let my mind dwell on Jesus and how wonderful He is. Then, ever so gently, the sensation came over me of being raised to a sitting position and being cradled in the arms of God! Then just as gently, I was swayed ever so slowly once to the left and once to the right; I was brought back to a sitting position. Again, oh ever so gently, my body was being tilted forward very slowly and then carefully back to the original position. The forward tilt was perhaps a thirty-five degrees. It was gentle, beautiful, and unexplainable. Without even having time to meditate upon the experience, I immediately fell asleep. Upon awakening Saturday morning and before anything had transpired, I had this definite compelling inclination to return home and attend choir practice at 10:00 a.m. that Saturday. I just couldn't understand it. (We aren't necessarily supposed to "understand," but to just do it.) I had come home to be with my mother for the weekend, and here I was being compelled to go back to choir practice.

When you are a child of the Holy Spirit, you know it, and when the Holy Spirit leads you, you know it. Well, I told my astonished mother that I must return, and so I did drive back. I simply could not understand it. Could you? During the speedy return trip, I again was experiencing the smell of sulfur! I was being purified and cleansed for the vision I was about to see, but naturally I didn't know that until later. Upon arriving at the church, I knelt down to pray and wait for the rest of the choir members. I was looking toward the altar and at the Crucifix. Suddenly all the glory of heaven began to radiate upon the body of Jesus hanging upon the cross. All the colors of the rainbow began to encompass the statue. The upper torso of Jesus was being enveloped with fluid gold. There were flashes of lightning, more rainbow glory, beautiful white and blue clouds, and more lightning, and then the statue of Jesus *"became as living flesh."* I was enraptured, caught up in glory. However, just prior to the beginning of the glory being unfolded before me, I became aware of a divine fragrance of incense—and yes, undeniably divine—the fragrance of Jesus enveloping me. It was as though I were being purified in a supernatural way for the glory to be unfolded before my eyes. Oh, the glory of the fragrance. It was perhaps somewhat like frankincense and myrrh. Indescribably divine! The vision may have lasted for several minutes, and I then became aware that another member of the choir had entered and also knelt down to pray. The vision ended.

After choir practice, I approached our choir director and quickly described the vision to her. I know she didn't believe me, but she did say, "How fascinating." How well I know just how difficult it is to believe in the supernatural for the average person, believer or nonbeliever alike. I really don't quite know why I shared with her, but God knows, and that's all I need to know. After practice I returned to my trailer, had lunch, and began to write a letter to my dear non-Christian friend in Phoenix (who was responsible for the mysterious way God had used her to bring about my attending the Kathryn Kuhlman service and my ultimate regeneration). Suddenly, I again began to smell the burning of sulfur, and again all I knew was that I must go back to the church! I couldn't reason why, but I simply was compelled to go back. A supernatural force (the Holy Spirit) was prompting me. By then it was approximately 2:30 p.m. Again, I entered the church, dropped to my knees, and began to pray. Again, the purifying divine incense encompassed and purified me for the vision. Again, the rainbow began enveloping and encompassing the Crucifix followed by lightning and more lightning, and then the flesh-like appearance of Jesus. How does one describe "glory"? I really don't know how long I knelt there watching this supernatural phenomenon. *Then, slowly and carefully, the huge Crucifix swayed from left to right* (just the exact motion as I had experienced the night before)—only one time *from left to right,* and then came to its previous upright position. Just as I had been tilted forward the night before, so too the Crucifix stopped, came to its original position, and then *began to tilt forward at quite a degree,* perhaps thirty-five to forty-degrees, and then just as carefully and slowly returned to the original position!

All this time I was not in a trance and I was not hypnotized; I simply had been a perfectly obedient child of God, kneeling and watching God unfold His supernatural power and wonder before my very eyes at 2:30 p.m. on a Saturday afternoon in the church. Later, when relating the experience to a Catholic sister, she said she felt that the "tilting forward" of the Crucifix (toward me) indicated that I would have a cross to bear in this life. She was right on in that statement, but at the same time, with the indwelling of God's Holy Spirit, I can carry my cross since I am yoked to Jesus. See Matthew 11:28–30, where Jesus is speaking: "Come to me, all you who are weary and burdened, and I will give you rest. Take my yoke upon you and learn from me, for I am gentle and humble in heart, and you will find rest for your souls. For my yoke is easy and my burden is light."

I am having a rough time; it's not all that easy being a good Christian. I am persecuted and ridiculed; I have some financial concerns; I have some health problems. But thank God, I am getting stronger and healthier with each passing day—both spiritually and physically. I am quite alone in a physical sense since I have no one to share these things with. It is extremely difficult to share deep spiritual revelations with just anyone. You must develop friendships with discernment, and if they are on the same plateau as you, they evidently have had experiences with the spiritual, and then you can share with each other. But regardless of everything, I now have eternal life, and I have and know the love of God, my Father, and the love of Jesus and the Holy Spirit. Nothing in this world can help me through all the tribulations except the knowledge I have of the power of Almighty God. Whatever is happening to me is for my own good and

God's glory. Physically, my body, just as yours, is aging every moment, but spiritually, I am growing in power and knowledge, and I will keep on growing for all eternity!

One evening after studying my Bible, playing my auto-harp, and singing to Jesus, I prepared for bed. In addition, after getting into bed, I spent some time talking to Jesus. It was such a beautiful way to relax and revel in the manifestations God had been revealing to me. I pondered and savored how good the Lord is, and ultimately fell sound asleep. Just how long I had slept, I really don't know, but for some inexplicable reason I was awakened and discovered the most exquisite fragrance enveloping the bedroom. It was pure and divine—not of this world, but an incomparable fragrance. I literally leaped out of bed, fell to my knees, and began to praise and worship the Lord. It was glorious. God has blessed me with this same phenomenon several more times, but never the powerful envelopment permeating the entire room as during the very first incident. This is the glorious fragrance, the essence of Jesus.

Another exciting phenomenon I was experiencing quite frequently was seeing auras above certain Christians' heads. I had been attending many charismatic meetings, and inexplicably, the lovely aura would appear around the heads of certain people. I wondered about it. Maybe these particular persons had been Spirit-filled in addition to being regenerated. Since the majority of persons attending these meetings were Christians, and so few had the auras, it puzzled me. Some Christians say that they are of the devil and a hangover from the old life. But since they are harmless, I just forget about it. If it is of the devil, he really works hard, doesn't he? You can be the judge. It has been quite some time since I have seen this manifestation, but when I least expect it, and never even give it a thought, there it is! It is really quite insignificant, but the fact remains that it is a supernatural phenomenon whether from good or evil. It is up to us to begin to discern spiritual manifestations as we grow. Mature Christians quite naturally say it's satanic. But I just praise God that I keep getting reminders of the authenticity of the wiles and ways of Satan!

Along the same line, you might be interested to know that Satan does attend Bible study group meetings on occasion. During one of our regular Bible study meetings, another supernatural, unexplainable event took place. We would always begin with a time of praying, singing, listening to tapes, studying the Bible, sharing experiences, etc. When I joined the group, there was one lady in particular that I was quite fascinated with, and I naïvely and innocently placed her upon a pedestal. I thought she was great. She knew her Bible too. We were in somewhat of a semicircular seating arrangement with the person teaching the study group at the head of the circle. (There were only ten to twelve of us.) I opened my Bible and glanced up at the teacher who was directly across the room from me; at that precise second, there appeared a green arch extending from the floor, up and around her head, and down to the floor on the other side of her chair. It was a green arch. Surprisingly, I didn't scream or fall off the chair, but I must admit I was stunned. This, at a Bible study group. What next?! It lasted several seconds, and just as quickly, it disappeared. I have never revealed to anyone who the woman was, even to this day—and to this day I am not certain why it happened, but I do have a childish idea. I, in my newborn state and spiritual naïveté, believed green stood for jealousy, and she was jealous of me because of the few supernatural happenings I selectively revealed to the group. We are supposed to "share" anything and almost everything to those with whom we are closely associated. As a result of that event, I eventually dropped out of the study group—perhaps three months later. I'm not positive of the time period, but it doesn't matter. I never returned. That supernatural phenomenon caused me to wonder about that woman, but more about myself![6]

Here is my present understanding. You see, Satan is curious about this type of meeting and pays an occasional visit to cause fear, doubt, and distrust. So he does the green arch bit. It raises thoughts in my mind, and unfortunately I drop out. One of the enemy's greatest weapons is to create dissension and division in any kind of a body of believers. He wanted me to leave the group because I was in the early stages of my new birth. He wanted to stunt my growth by causing me to question and then drop out. Child that I was, it amazes me to think anyone would be jealous of me. Satan simply didn't want me to attend Bible study as I was learning more and more about him and his rotten tactics, especially with newborn believers. He wants to isolate baby Christians from the more mature Christians. He doesn't want any Christians to reach maturity because they are beginning to understand the enemy and what to do about protecting themselves from his arrows of deceit. They become a threat to Satan, and he hates them because of it.

God never reveals the nature of anyone to us in an extraordinary manner because we, being immature, would perhaps begin to flex our undeveloped discernment and irrationally "judge" him. That is God's job, not ours. On the other hand, paradoxically, God does have control over Satan, and I asked myself why God allowed Satan to make that unscheduled appearance. It did cause me minor concern for approximately one year. What was God trying to teach me? Certainly God did not want me to drop out of the study group—but the enemy did, and I did drop out. Naturally I began more diligently to make up for that loss in other ways.

Another interesting experience occurred prior to my leaving the study group—another puzzling, still unanswered enigma. Here we go. After returning home from one of the study groups, I began to leaf through one of the Christian magazines I brought home from the study. Again, *I didn't expect anything supernatural! I never do!* I was standing next to the kitchen table, just quickly leafing through the magazine. Suddenly, my eyes were drawn to the blinking of a *square* light about the size of a postage stamp that was over an application form about the size of a three-by-five card in most business offices. I said out loud, "I don't believe it!" I began to laugh, perhaps nervously—what on earth was going on? Am I cracking up, slowly cracking up? The square light continued to blink on and off on the application form. I can't remember what I was saying to myself, but I believe I must have said, "Lord, do You want me to fill out that application as a candidate for the Christian Peace Corps?" No answer. Finally the light began to shine, telling me to sit down and fill out the form. I obeyed. I sat down and filled it out, and then cut it out of the magazine. Then and only then did the blinking cease. As I am telling you about this, it still baffles me—this activity. I don't think I shared this with more than a few close persons. I was already learning what "they" would say.

And my dear readers, by now you too must be saying to yourselves, "I never heard of such goings on. It's just unbelievable! It can't be real!" Let's recap thus far:

1) The first and greatest supernatural experience was, of course, my new birth (which took place on the bus going to California to attend the Kathryn Kuhlman service), when I was literally born of God's Spirit and my dead spirit was regenerated. To date I know of nothing to compare this to. I will live forever with God in His Kingdom, forever and ever.

2) I attended the Kathryn Kuhlman meeting when I actually was overshadowed by the Holy Spirit during the time I was seated in the audience, and the Holy Spirit's presence began to cause me to tremble and

shake like a leaf tossed about in a wind storm.

3) Then I was slain in the Spirit, and then fell to the floor after I had given my testimony before ten thousand people while in an unexplainable euphoria.

4) After arising from the floor in humble awareness as God was beginning to awaken me from my dead state, I was beginning to realize just how great and omnipotent our God is!

5) I returned to Miss Kuhlman again to beseech her to pray for me that I wouldn't go bald, was slain in the Spirit again (the second time), and upon awakening, experienced tumultuous racing through my mind.

6) And finally, when I sat up from the second slaying, my eyes gazed toward Miss Kuhlman. The supernatural drawing of my eyes heavenward caused me to see two streams of fire piercing time to further activate my soul into an awareness of God's power—the instant realization that my soul was laid bare, exposed before God in all its nakedness. I knew at that moment that God knew *everything* about me, and I could never hide from *Him*. At that climactic moment, I was enslaved and branded a prisoner of God's love for me.

From the recapping of the above events to the present, encompassing a period of approximately one year, no more further supernatural activity took place until I returned to Pennsylvania, joined the Bible study group, and experienced the incident of the baffling "blinking light." However, since I was now a regenerated spirit being, I was being exposed to supernatural spiritual events; and whether I realized it or not, I was growing spiritually in the way that God had determined for me to grow.

If you had been in my shoes, how do you think you would have reacted? How would you express these happenings to unbelieving people (not all)? Would you have kept it all locked up inside yourself? What do you think you would have done? As I have explained to you before, I determined again and again to try to hear God speaking to me, studying with all diligence to try to do the will of God as I understood Him. This leads me to the point where I emphatically do believe with all my heart that the Holy Spirit prompted me with great conviction to share these events with you. What would be the point in keeping it all to myself? Prayerfully, perhaps many of you who read this book will be motivated to read the Book of Books, the Holy Bible, and by the leading of the Holy Spirit you will be inspired to take that vital step of asking Jesus into your life and heart.

Now let's return to the phenomenon of the "blinking light." I mailed the application to the Christian Peace Corps in Washington, D.C., and received a prompt reply by a personal telephone call from the director of the Corps. She asked several questions, especially what caused me to respond to the application. I told her of the blinking light. Her response was, "That is just the beginning. God will continue to manifest His glory to you as long as you continue to abide in Jesus Christ." She further explained to me that a battery of tests would be forthcoming, and I was to ask one of the professors at the college to preside over the examination. After the results were mailed back, it wasn't long before I received confirmation that I was accepted for the Christian Peace Corps (and she also informed me that I was the first Catholic they had ever accepted) if I could meet the following requirement. It was absolute policy that my church must support me while I was in the Corps. Well, since I had arrived in Pennsylvania and had attended a Catholic church for only several months before dropping out, I really didn't belong to any church. I was still searching for a church where my spiritual needs would be fulfilled, and so the problem was not resolved at that particular time. Also, I received words of advice from several members of the Bible study group I had attended who warned me that the blinking light could be one way of Satan deceiving me since I was just a baby toddling Christian. Since the monetary issue could not be resolved (I was willing to pay the monthly fee myself, but that simply could not be done), the incident must not have been of God. Again, I don't know if the light was from God or Satan. If it was from God, again I let Him down. If it was from the enemy, the devil, God blocked his subterfuge and prevented me from getting into something I really wasn't spiritually prepared to handle as a new born again Christian. So you see, the learning process continues and will continue from here into eternity.

The days are quickly passing by. My routine doesn't change: study, study, study the Bible unceasingly; praise and sing to the Lord; prayer time and talk time with Jesus—ever yearning, ever longing to know my Jesus more and more. By this time, you should be prepared for just about anything I reveal to you, and I must have been more prepared than I actually realized, or God would not have allowed it to happen. One night I was suddenly awakened out of a sound sleep—and there at the foot of my bed, as though suspended from the ceiling, were two ugly, luminous shiny heads. The facial features were humanistic, but horribly distorted—ugly demons. I suppose if I weren't in bed, I would have fallen in a dead faint. Needless to say, I was almost—let me repeat, almost—stunned by the sight. Immediately I said what I had learned way back in Phoenix just after my new birth: "Satan, in the name of Jesus, I command you to leave this instant, for greater is *He* who is within me than you who are in the world." Instantly they disappeared. Why the demons? I do believe that God was allowing me to see that they really exist. (Remember that Jesus' early ministry and to the end was spent in casting out demons—many, many, many demons.) And I suppose I did believe they did exist, but probably as deeply as I believed in fairies. Perhaps I did have reservations just as you have, but my Father wanted me to know unequivocally that they really do exist. What a revelation. And I really was not frightened—just caught by surprise! After all, and believe me, I now have faith (out of sheer necessity) in myself with the power of the Holy Spirit, in the name of Jesus to "cast out demons." (I pray that I will never be called upon to do it, but if I must, I will.) Mark 16:17: "And these signs shall follow them that believe; In my name shall they cast out devils; they shall speak with new tongues" (kjv). Jesus spoke those words to those who were gathered with Him on the Mount of Olives just before He ascended into heaven.

Life went on. Strangely, I again began to feel somehow, something was still missing. What was it? This constant, ever present compulsion of something lacking haunted me. One cold December day, it came to my mind that I had never been immersed totally in water baptism. I had been sprinkled as a baby when I was only eight or ten days old. Jesus was thirty years old when He was water baptized by John the Baptist in total immersion and received the infilling of the Holy Spirit as He came up out of the Jordan River. That clearly sent a signal to me that you have to make your own decision regarding baptism. Water baptism is a decision you make when you recognize that you and you alone are responsible for your sins and prayerfully are baptized. You don't have any sins when you are a ten-day-old baby, but when you reach the age of accountability and sorrowfully repent of your sins, you accept the act of being water baptized. You are dead and buried just as Jesus was and then are coming up out of the water death, totally resurrected into a new creation. That was what the Holy Spirit had been trying to impress upon me for almost two years. I could hardly contain myself until I, too, was baptized by total immersion for the remission of my sins. As I am learning, baptism should usually follow the new birth within as close a time as possible. No, you don't *have to be baptized in water* to enter heaven, but you should, as a Christian, learn the basic fundamental teachings of this incredible new life following our Lord and Master.

It was an extremely cold day in January 1975 when I heard of a baptism being held in a small town approximately thirty miles away. There were only five of us. One of the men who was going to be baptized told me he had seen "Jesus." Oh me. That man was in complete awe of Jesus and was overwhelmed with love for the Savior. His actions, his attitude, his entire demeanor completely verified the beautiful revelation of our Savior. I was not then totally aware of the profoundness of the act of total immersion baptism, but I *obediently* followed the command: "*Repent*, and be baptized every one of you in the name of Jesus Christ for the remission of sins, and ye shall receive the gift of the Holy Ghost" (Acts 2:38 kjv, emphasis added). Also see and read for yourselves Acts 8:36–40 and Luke 3:16–17. There is so much to learn, to know, and to receive.

Just about the time the things begin to level off a little—God is so gracious to me and wants me to be happy and enjoy life—He sovereignly reveals something new to me—joy, joy, joy. Believe me, there is nothing boring or dull in being a believer, a Christian. One plateau of growth inevitably takes the believer on to another plateau, and then another—you can never get enough spiritual food to satisfy you; it is infinite. And with the *obedient* act of baptism, I eagerly embraced—again, I had reached another fulfillment of unfathomable peace and quiet joy. It was done; the compulsion (leading of the Holy Spirit) had been accomplished. Praise God!

Chapter 5

The Mystery Guest

O ne day in the mailbox was my monthly newsletter from the Full Gospel Businessmen's Fellowship International (FGBMFI). The highlight mentioned a forthcoming trip to the Bahamas. Anyone wishing to make the trip was to complete the enclosed reservation form and return it to the FGBMFI office in the area. Yes, you surmised correctly: I felt an extremely overwhelming desire to go with the group. I couldn't escape it; I just had to make the trip. The meeting point was Miami, Florida, where we would board our ship and cruise lazily to the Bahamas. My one great desire was to be with these zealous, turned-on Christians. The purpose of the trip was to honor and lift up Jesus, to evangelize, to enjoy the relaxing cruise, to eat to our heart's desire on board ship, to do some sightseeing and some shopping in Nassau, and to bask in the fellowship of believers. The literature indicated there was to be quite an impressive group of speakers. Well, it didn't take me but a split second to make the decision to go. I contacted my sister. Would she care to go along? Yes, but I was not to press her in any way with my unquenchable fervor.

She wanted to sightsee and shop. Out of due respect, she would attend one, or at the most two, of the seminars on board ship. We had much excited planning. And finally the day of departure arrived.

Now is a good time to examine the contents of the brochure. It gave all specifics of the places we were going to visit, the dates, an agenda of the meetings to be held on board the ship, and finally a gallery of pictures of all the speakers except one. I do believe the number of speakers was six. Their names were naturally given, plus a few interesting relevant facts of their backgrounds, *except* for the one blank frame. No name was given; however, several statements were made about the individual—the most exciting fact being that he, a Jew, had accepted Jesus as his Messiah! That is always exciting to any Christian, and I was eagerly looking forward to this "mystery guest's" testimony! They booked him because he was Jewish, was born in Israel, and would be a wonderful testimony to the Jewish people who were still "looking for their Messiah." This person would be the second Jewish born again believer I had ever met. Of course, I was thrilled.

The time was 2:00 p.m., on a beautiful sunny day on board the S.S. *Emerald Seas* cruise ship. There were 100 to 150 of us fervent believers on board. We sang (a high form of praising God), prayed, sang some more, and finally settled down to hear what the Master of Ceremonies had to offer. I do not remember the order of the speakers, but the "mystery guest" was given quite an exciting introduction by the M.C. He explained to us that because of the possible negative repercussions that might be inflicted on the mystery guest, they hadn't revealed his name in the brochure to protect him as much as possible. Again, the M.C. stated the guest was born in Israel. And it is common knowledge that when a Jewish person does accept Jesus as his Messiah, there is a lot of discord within the family, and on many occasions, the family will cut all ties with the completed Jewish person. Well, whatever information was given was minimal since the guest himself was standing nearby to give "his testimony" of his conversion and meeting of Jesus the Messiah.

The "mystery guest" approached the microphone and introduced himself. I was literally holding my breath. I was all ears. I was highly excited to hear what he had to share. Praise the Lord! Then, before he had his name out of his mouth, my *ears* were suddenly and totally blocked. I couldn't hear a thing. I was totally oblivious to the fact that I was on board ship, harbored at Nassau (1975), at 2:00 p.m., on a glorious, beautiful day, with a group of 100 to 150 believers. I was ware of *nothing* but the man on stage. *I did not hear one word of his testimony;* I don't know how long he spoke, although I suspect it was perhaps only five minutes or so. That really isn't important. I could not hear; I was perplexed and asked, "Lord, why can't I hear? I came on this trip primarily to listen to the testimony of this Jewish born again man." *At that precise moment,* something so tremendous happened that to this day I am still overwhelmed by it all—a beautiful, handsome spirit man stepped out from the body of the mystery guest! If I hadn't been under the power of the Holy Spirit, unquestionably I would have shrieked, jumped up, or anything; but as it was, I was sort of transfixed, paralyzed, frozen stiff, mute—whatever. I did nothing, and I am certain I wouldn't have done anything even if I could! Just as subtly as the spirit stepped forward one step outside of the body of the mystery guest, he (the spirit) stepped backward one step and reentered his body. For a split nanosecond, I wondered, "What on earth?" when again, very subtly, the spirit man again stepped forward one step out from the body of the mystery guest.

At this point, my mental faculties began to function with, "Check the spirit," and so I did. What I noted on this second appearance was that the spirit was dressed in clothing similar to the attire of the Mideast Arabs, Muslims, etc.

The spirit man had on a long, off-white robe with vertical, wide, black stripes extending to the floor; the shade of the toga was as discernible as the dark color of the goatee. The spirit had on a turban. The turban was also off-white with black stripes and with flaps that extended almost down to his shoulders (similar to the old French Foreign Legionnaires). He was of olive complexion, similar to the Mideast people. His *eyes* were in a downcast position. How I thank God for that! His hands were clasped together and extended casually to their full length in front of his body. Then subtly he again stepped one step backward and reentered the body of the mystery guest. (Exclamation!)

I really didn't have time to do or think anything in the transfixed state I was in. I must have blinked my eyes, and then the spirit man stepped one step forward out of the mystery guest's body for the *third* and final time. Very swiftly, I took in all the specific identification features to make certain I had it all correctly photographed in my mind. Evidently, I had done a good job and quickly ran the checklist of the first two appearances. The inventory again was as follows: he (the spirit man) was handsome; he was slender in build and probably 5?10˝ tall; he had a dark goatee (this I noted in the third appearance); generally speaking, his facial features were quite normal and unremarkable in appearance; his complexion was a lovely olive tone. His robe was off-white with vertical black stripes extended to the floor; his turban was also off-white and black striped, with flaps extending almost to his shoulders; and his hands were clasped in front of his body, extending to their full length. The three appearances had not changed in any detail. God made sure I took in everything necessary by having the appearance of the spirit three times! God is so great! While still in the power of the Holy Spirit, my first deep impression (discernment) was that the spirit was Arabic or Jewish. I'm generally quite slow on the pickup, if you know what I mean, and God really has to draw pictures for me because I am that way. But praise God, now I am elated that I am naïve and childlike because I have so much more revealed to me. I am a student, and the Holy Spirit is my teacher guide. Two of His most outstanding features are His gentleness and, of course, His patience.

Now, paradoxically, the Jewish mystery guest *did not* have the beautiful olive complexion of the majority of the Mideast people. In fact, this mystery guest was of extremely fair complexion, like a Dane or Swede; he also had blond hair; he was not slender, but actually somewhat on the stocky side, to be exact. *Now are you getting the picture?* If this spirit that emerged out of the mystery guest's body was his own spirit, it would have been an exact duplicate of his physical body, from what I have heard to be a fundamental teaching within Christianity. Therefore, the spirit emanating from the mystery man was *not* his spirit man. But then whose spirit was indwelling the mystery guest?

Naturally I spent deep prayer time on it, but I *did not dwell on it.* God does not "give" visions indiscriminately, and it was given to me for some specific purpose. God knew exactly how many seconds the mystery guest would be speaking, so God programmed the three appearances right down to the last nanosecond. The mystery man had finished his testimony, and I had not heard a single word. People began applauding, and the vision was over. Did God orchestrate the vision, or did the devil? As you are now aware, these spiritual challenges are given to develop our spirituality to the extent willed by God Almighty.

Needless to say, I kept the vision bottled up inside me until that evening in our stateroom when I just had to share it with my sister or explode. You just cannot keep an experience of that magnitude capped up very long. And, of course, God knew that was exactly what I would do. My sister's reaction was what I had expected, and she did stare at me rather strangely, to say the least. Naturally, she had no comment. But by this time, I was becoming indoctrinated to that other dimension, and again I reacted somewhat quietly and mystified as to this revelation of revelations.

The following evening, I cornered one of the officers of the FGBMFI and related the same story I had told my sister. He questioned me briefly; he asked me how I felt during the vision and if I was frightened. I replied that I was not frightened and I didn't feel anything. I was rather numb. We dwelled on the subject for only a short time, had a prayer regarding it all, and then went our separate ways. I did pray about the vision several times in the next four years, but God has not chosen to reveal to me who the spirit was. Talk about suspense! God does love to do things when you *least* expect it—He sort of takes you by surprise. I simply couldn't even dream of such an event! Isn't God simply fantastic? Didn't your physical father ever surprise you completely? Well, God is my spiritual Father, and He loves me dearly—and I believe He plans my surprises very lovingly and carefully, and of course He alone knows the reason and outcome.

Our trip was all over all too soon; we returned to the states. I was back to work as usual, but I was quite aglow over the vision given to me by God. Why, Lord, were You exalting me with these experiences? I say the vision was given by God because Satan would be dividing his own house if he revealed something negative, right? Upon sharing the vision with a very select few Christians, their response was, "Watch out—it probably was from Satan!" Well, if I am wrong in my assumption, no harm done—and if it was from Satan, he was defeating whatever purpose he had in mind. As a result of the vision, I spent even more time seeking God; more time in earnest, fervent prayer; more time in studying the Word; and more time in singing and playing my autoharp in worship and praise to God in song. Actually, I think Satan is a little more clever than that. Also, whatever Satan does is strictly to lead us very subtly into evil. This was just the reverse.

As a point of coincidental interest, the vision just described was exactly two years later than the first one I experienced at the church. I naïvely and foolishly thought that perhaps a vision pattern was emerging, but of course, that simply was not the case. God's ways are diverse and infinite, as I am learning in my day-to-day living.

The days are passing by, the months all too swiftly. I ponder the vision seriously two or three times a year. I am only human—you would too, wouldn't you? I pray at those times for God to reveal what it all means if it is His will, and if He chooses not to reveal what it means, it is perfectly all right with me. At least I feel prepared for the outcome, whatever it is. Possibly a full year had passed, and I began to sense faint stirrings within my spirit to seek something more, but what should I seek? What else was there left for me to do? I was puzzled and tried to pass it off as my imagination, but then imagination is something I do not possess.

Dear friend, I worked in an office of three highly intelligent men who could assure you that I don't have an ounce of imagination; it just shows. At one point, however, one of them made the statement that we "could see" anything we really wanted to see by deep concentration. Well, I cannot even imagine what a peanut looks like. Maybe those who are highly intellectual can conjure up something like a vision (but in my humble opinion, I think they would need a little assistance such as angel dust, etc.), but I am not a highly intellectual person. They would testify to that—rather, I am just an average, normal being but extremely sensitive to almost everything—and now I must add the spirit world! (Born again, alive spirit.)

The mystifying "stirrings" within my soul increased. As usual, I studied the Bible more diligently than before, prayed for more light, and tried to "hear" what the Holy

Spirit was saying—all to no avail, until one day I had an inspiration to go into my tiny den and look for "something" to re-read. I have read some of my favorite books three and four times—those that especially appealed to my nature. Some of my favorite authors are David du Plessis (the father of Pentecostalism), Robert Frost, David Wilkerson, Kenneth Hagin, Kenneth Copeland, Pat Robertson of the *700 Club,* Don Basham, Watchman Nee, Mel Tari, Charles Capps, T. Austin Sparks, C.S. Lewis, Dr. Charles Taylor, Paul E. Billheimer, and the deeply spiritual books of Francis Schaeffer (which I hardly understand). I have read all of Dr. Taylor's books dealing primarily with prophecy—my favorite subject. Then there are Theodore H. Epp; John E. Walvoord; M.R. DeHann, M.D.; T.L. Osborn; Tim LaHaye; A.B. Simpson; and I am certain many of you have read the quite sensational *666* (dealing with the mark of the beast) and the provocative *1000 Year Millennium* authored by Salem Kirban, a born again Arab. The list goes on and on, and all the books are written by Christian authors.

The sifting, sorting, and checking continued—now with compelling urgency. I knew I simply must find a certain book—but which one, and why? After searching for perhaps fifteen to twenty minutes, I selected a book written by Salem Kirban (an Arab as mentioned above). Instantly I knew *The Millennium* was what I had been searching for! Don't ask me how, but I just knew it! Slowly and deliberately (and I might add, cautiously—after all, anything can happen and usually does), I began leafing through the book. I was unconsciously looking for something, but I didn't have a clue what it was. There were perhaps five to ten pages of pictures relating to the story. Slowly I kept thumbing page after page after page, *and suddenly*—there it was—that certain something I had been searching for but didn't know what it was! What a dilemma. Let me state that the entire novel was based on selected scriptures relevant to the novel.

This one was written and enhanced in such a stimulating manner as to make it a most entertaining, intriguing, and thought-provoking book for the average non-Christian to read. For instance, in the novel, we are projected in time to the year 2000 a.d. Air transportation is vastly accelerated; a flight directly to Israel from New York would perhaps take only an hour or so. Technology in every aspect of living had increased beyond imagination (especially in the field of computers). The novel is very exciting, and the author could reap a fortune if he sold the rights to Hollywood to make a film (I believe).

Now sharpen up your imaginations as we get to the meat of the story. In the picture, the star figure is standing (the entire novel is about the anti-Christ named Brother Bartholomew and his reign on earth during the seven-year tribulation as recorded in the Bible in the end times). Kneeling at the feet of Brother Bartholomew and kissing his hand is another figure. But in the murky background is a *third figure.* At first glance, I detected nothing extraordinary at all about the scene since I had read the book at least three times and merely glossed over the pictures. However, suddenly I was strongly prompted to take a second look at the third figure in the background. *This was it!* I was jubilant— the cork of the champagne bottle had been "popped." The *figure* in the murky background—are you ready, readers— was almost an exact likeness of the spirit man I had seen in the vision on board ship a year or so earlier. The two figures were ninety-eight percent identical. The figure in the murky background in the novel was the personage of the false prophet. He had all the same facial characteristics as the spirit man who emerged from the body of the mystery guest and without question could be considered his twin. To explain the two percent lacking, there were two glitches: 1) the false prophet in the novel was wearing a robe similar to the spirit man who emerged from the mystery guest, except it did not have wide, black, vertical stripes; 2) the false prophet in the novel had his arms extended at his sides rather than in front of his body. Other than these two glitches, the personages are almost one hundred percent identical. This almost identical appearance in the novel is what caused me to come to a screeching halt when I noticed the outstanding similarities of the facial features and not what they were wearing. Twins look alike by facial features, not clothes.

What can I say further at this point? I was very quiet and subdued. My spiritual eyes had been opened again. But why did all this happen in the first place? Can you not see from all I have written thus far that I naïvely accepted with much eagerness and anticipation the opportunity of going on my first cruise as just a mini-vacation—never, never, never dreaming of what was going to transpire. The most compelling factor and added bonus to this trip, however, was the exciting fact that I was going to meet a completed Jewish man—my first ever. Yet, I am positive the Holy Spirit was leading and prompting me throughout this exciting adventure. And I am just as positive that it was the Holy Spirit causing the restless stirrings within my soul to search my books to find the answer to my query: "Who was the spirit man who emerged from the body of the mystery guest on the cruise to the Bahamas?" Upon finally finding "the picture," I immediately noticed that the restless stirring of my soul was divinely quieted. I was now experiencing total peace and knew definitely that no further searching was necessary. I had, indeed, discovered what the Holy Spirit had been prompting me to look for. Praise the Lord! Truly I can see the hand of God in this adventure. Or do you feel that my naïveté is being exploited by the devil? Only God knows, and time will tell all. But only God and His omniscience knew *exactly* to the split second the length of time the mystery guest would need to give his testimony, and God spaced the three appearances of the spirit to exactly use the very last second. That's my Father,

Abba, the Great and Holy God. Words are so futile. I am thrilled and constantly amazed at His omniscience, omnipotence, and omnipresence. And as they say, we haven't seen anything yet! I can hardly wait until I get to Heaven; I have many questions to ask my Father. But in the meantime, I am learning to wait, to be patient, to be loving, and to learn of Jesus, knowing that the answer to everything will be revealed at the time that God so wills. I am very, very contented.

Upon returning home from the Bahamas, I naturally sought my sister in Christ who lived across the road from me. After relating the happenings on the trip, I asked her to pray for some light with regard to the event. She did pray— and after meditating awhile on the vision, she responded that the mystery guest was perhaps not quite what he claimed to be. (Most of us aren't what we appear to be either.) Her answer was sufficient for the time being, but I mulled over it, prayed about it, and earnestly endeavored to come to a spiritual solution as to what it meant—but alas, to no avail. Then I simply stored away the whole scenario in my memory bank for future contemplation and decided again to concentrate more deeply on my study of the Bible.

About a year later, I flew to Florida for a much-needed vacation. While I was there, I decided to visit Gerald Derstine's Christian Retreat. My sister in Christ, mentioned above, told me about the Retreat and thought that perhaps it would be a nice place for me to spend several days of my vacation. I did, and I had such a relaxing time that I spent all ten days of my vacation there rather than just the three originally planned. At the Retreat, a three-month Bible study course was in progress, a sort of "crash course" in the study of God and man. I attended most of the meetings since it appeared that was what the Great Holy Spirit had ordered for me.

Now, get ready! Coincidentally (?) I just happened to encounter a person at the Retreat who had been one of the speakers on board the ship on our trip to the Bahamas. Are you still with me? Are you in the least bit getting curious? Finally, I was able to approach him during one of the meals and told him how delighted I was to be at the Retreat and especially of meeting him personally. Naturally, I especially wanted to talk to him about the "mystery guest" during the Bahamas trip. I went into all details just as I have shared with you. He made several responses to statements I had made and then said, "I invited that man some time ago to give his testimony at a local church meeting. I didn't 'feel' right about that man—there was something wrong about him; I sensed it in my spirit. But, of course, I didn't know what." Also, he revealed to me that the "mystery guest" was having all kinds of financial problems, had lost a lucrative business, and was returning to Israel, defeated. But readers, Christians, true Christians, should not and do not turn back. This unfortunate person did "turn back"—end of scenario.

My sister in Christ with whom I shared my trip was witness number one that the man could be an imposter; the person I met at the Retreat said, "There was something definitely negative about the mystery man"—witness number two. When you have two witnesses with similar versions of an incident, you are said to have a valid case against a person who is guilty of committing an illegal act or whatever the situation might be. Consequently, I know now for a fact that all "mystery guests" of the FGBMFI meetings will be thoroughly checked as to whether or not they have been truly "born again." It is a frightening thing to try to play games with God.

The fact that God simplified the whole scene of the vision for me is exactly the way God works with me. I never in a thousand years could have determined what the vision meant, but God simply referred me to the book *The Millennium*. The "picture" of the three figures said in essence, "There is your answer." My dear readers, you get the whole picture, don't you? The mystery man is a "false personage"—now to what degree, I have no idea. At times, I have listened for the Holy Spirit to go further in this matter, but as yet, nothing. I know who the man is and what his line of business was. I easily can get his name (but do not feel it is necessary at this time); he is on record in the files of the FGBMFI as being a "mystery guest" on that particular cruise of believers to the Bahamas. If God leads me, I shall be obedient. I have prayed for and about the person, but without really knowing just exactly what to specifically pray for. He definitely has a foreign spirit within him, and I do believe that false spirit has got to go. I am waiting for the Holy Spirit to guide me.

Before retiring one evening while still at the Retreat, I asked my hostess and a friend of hers to pray with me after the evening service; I had no particular reason, but just wanted to acknowledge and worship God. We did. Immediately upon going to my room, I again knelt in prayer. I was full of joy, love, and peace. Generally speaking, "All was well, very well with my soul." While in prayer, I suddenly became aware of a "wheel of fire" spinning around my body. I was enthralled and continued in prayer. Then as mysteriously as the wheel appeared, it suddenly spun upward, upward, and then completely disappeared.

The next morning I shared with my hostess what had occurred, and she had no explanation other than perhaps I had been "delivered of something." But that was conjecture on her part. If that is the case, I would like to be delivered more frequently in that spectacular manner, but it has never happened again. Spiritual, supernatural— the more you kneel in prayer and commune with God in your spirit, the more He will reveal the supernatural to you. The supernatural, spiritual world is very much alive and doing exceedingly well! You see, if you truly are born again, regenerated, it is only reasonable to believe you will "see" things in the spiritual world of which you are now a full member as a spiritual child of God.

Does God want me to visit that "mystery" person and "cast out" the foreign spirit? Evidently not, or the Holy Spirit would guide me. Yet, just why did God allow this to happen to me—a test? Undoubtedly, God knows exactly what I will or will not do. God may have given this particular assignment to some other person who failed the test and then gave it to me. So on that assumption, perhaps *I am doing* something by sharing the event to other believers to give them something to fall back on, if in fact they at some time have a spiritual experience.

Is Satan trying to make a fool of me so I will be ridiculed by my acquaintances? Maybe. But what I can state positively (with God as my Judge) is that everything happened as I have recorded it to you. Did God want me to reveal all these supernatural experiences? I truly think so. But if Satan did have a hand in this, I can praise God because I am made even more aware of the spiritual world in accordance with the will of God. My spiritual muscles certainly are being exercised; I am ever growing and developing spiritually; my faith is strong as I constantly am in the Word. I am confident of the future and of my knowledge of Jesus Christ; I am alive forevermore. Praise God!

Chapter 6

The Lovely Name of Jesus

*fter rereading this entire document and having been obedient to what the Holy Spirit impressed upon me to write, now is the time to reveal some of the divine healings I have experienced. Three to five years ago, I had been suffering from chronic bladder infections. The pain was devastating, and I would shrink in fear when the first symptoms would appear and instantly would resort to prayer and medication. "On one occasion after having visited with my mother, and on the way back home, the bladder infection symptoms began to manifest within my body. Upon reaching home I discovered to my horror that I had no medication." At this point I sank to my knees to pray. The pain continued with such intensity that I had to lie down on the floor in complete submission to the pain. I was in terror and began to call on the name of Jesus. "Jesus, help me, dear Lord." Softly and ever so gently, I gradually began to feel tender divine waves of healing pulsating throughout my body. My assurance began ascending as my fear was diminishing; calling on the lovely name of Jesus consoled me. The healing continued perhaps for three or four minutes. The acute agony began to subside, and at last there was absolutely no pain at all. Jesus, our compassionate and precious Savior, apparently rescues us when we absolutely do not know how to deal with such a situation and especially when we are absolutely alone. I had no one to turn to except Jesus, and how I praised and thanked Him for His gentle touch. I cannot recall whether or not I "resisted" the devil; I simply was in such pain that I could not think coherently. I called upon the lovely name of Jesus who is always with me, and He in tenderness and love responded to my call.

As you are discovering, one of the first lessons a new believer *must* learn is to quote scripture to resist the enemy's attacks. If you are just a baby and your faith is not sufficiently developed, the enemy knows it and refuses to oblige. It is at such moments that I resort to Jesus, and because He understands my lack of faith, He lovingly comes to the rescue. But it is up to us to develop as rapidly as possible; Jesus expects us to and wants us to begin to exercise our understanding and authority and to do battle with the enemy as real Christian soldiers. Isaiah 53:5 states, "But he was wounded for our transgressions, he was bruised for our iniquities: the chastisement of our peace was upon him; and with his stripes we are healed" (kjv).

Sinus attacks or migraine headaches have been a curse and blessing to me during my entire adult life. It seemingly is an inherent weakness from my mother. From the time I was a child, I can remember that she had a covering of some sort on her head as she suffered excruciatingly with sinus or migraine attacks. I have been blessed with the same thing. I say "blessed" because if I didn't have the attacks, I probably would not seek God as often. So as I suffer, I seek God and

His Word and practice my faith by flexing my spiritual muscles. If we didn't suffer, we wouldn't have the opportunity to practice our faith, would we? As this growing up process is quite painful but necessary, we must practice what we know is true. If we don't have enough faith to pray effectively for ourselves, we certainly won't be able to effectively pray for anyone else.

Back to the sinus/migraine attacks—they would be so intense in nature that I believe "withdrawal" from drugs, from what I have read and understand, would be somewhat comparable. The scenario begins with a pounding headache that increases in pressure and mounting intensity as the minutes go by. Ultimately, the threshold is reached in a crescendo of screaming agony, and suddenly I would begin to violently throw up; then dry heaves, convulsive heaves; then at last, incredible blessed relief. The entire cycle takes six to ten hours; complete recovery of strength would take at least forty-eight hours before I was back to normal. I don't know why I was allowed to suffer so horribly. I would beg for death or at least unconsciousness, but to no avail. Once the cycle began, there was no way of stopping it. Thank God I have not had such an attack for four or five years. On occasion when symptoms began to appear, if I resisted Satan and nothing happened, I would in desperation call on Jesus. Sometimes I would be healed within minutes, but at other times I would have a splitting headache for several days but no more going through the whole cycle. Thankfully, I have begun to notice much more physical strength in my body to withstand pain, and at the same time I also notice that as my faith and trust in Jesus are growing, so the pain diminishes. I praise and thank God for whatever happens as my understanding and faith increase by what the Holy Word of God teaches me. Romans 5:3–5: "Not only so, but we also rejoice in our sufferings, because we know that suffering produces perseverance; perseverance, character; and character, hope.

And hope does not disappoint us, because God has poured out his love into our hearts by the Holy Spirit, whom he has given us."

In lesser calamities such as burns, for instance, it seems to me to be mind over matter, but it isn't—I softly call on Jesus and simply ask Him not to let me feel the burn. Yes, He keeps me from feeling the pain. I could have killed myself several times crawling on ladders or slipping and sliding down basement stairs on my back, but somehow my Guardian Angel has kept me from serious accidents. You begin to know when God's mercy takes over.

So, I do know for certain that through it all Jesus has been with me, encouraging me to go on, one day at a time. That is my daily prayer: "Just be with me this day, precious Jesus." Jesus is my total strength; He carries the greater weight of my trials and burdens. I am learning every day, and yet the more I learn, the more I know I have yet to learn because I really don't know much of anything except that I know Jesus.

When we are born again, all our sins are forgiven and we are clothed with the righteousness of Jesus. God sees us as "righteousness" because we have accepted His Son as our Redeemer. Now, our sins are forgiven, right? But it says in the Bible, "Whatsoever a man soweth, that shall he also reap" (Galatians 6:7 kjv). That is a divine principle and cannot be broken. With regard to my sufferings, yes, I know beyond a shadow of a doubt that I have been cleansed by His precious blood and have been forgiven. But at the same time, God's divine laws cannot be annulled, so I truly believe that I am reaping what I had sown. So I gird myself up daily, putting on the full armor of God, praying more, studying the Word more, and practicing my faith more (loving all). I know that I am over the hump. More and more, the tortuous nightmares of physical agony are at last a thing of minor consequence, and with God's grace I am able to endure. I unceasingly thank and praise God for His great compassion on this born again child. I am learning that I can endure all things through Christ Jesus.

The most supreme area of my relationship with God is the exquisite communion with Him when I am in prayer. This spiritual communion is holy, divine, inexpressible—the essence of purity, the complete rapture of my spirit when in communion with God. Words are futile and my heart pours out love, adoration, and worship to my precious Lord Jesus who made it all possible with His infinite love for me and for all those who would seek Him. He ever cares for you and will respond to your love in seeking Him. Hallelujah! Call now on the lovely name of Jesus. There is no other to save you, except Him.

Summary and Conclusion

*T*he preceding events were to me, of course, the most astounding major highlights of my new birth (regeneration), and I hope they have given hope to you, my dear friends. There have been, and still are ongoing, many degrees of spiritual revelations given to me, and they will continue as long as I live in Christ Jesus.

Naturally, my spirituality continues to develop day by day because I feed on the Word, which is the only source of spiritual development.

1) Prior to the born again experience, I was spiritually dead and therefore never experienced anything spiritual.

2) After my born again experience, my life was entirely turned around; the things I once enjoyed tremendously, I now hated intensely—to the point of loathing.

3) Before I was spiritually regenerated, I was looking only to the physical. Now that I have been spiritually regenerated, I look to the spiritual unceasingly. Even though I am in the world, I am not of the world. I am

a physical being living in a physical world *and* a regenerated spiritual entity living also in the spiritual dimension—I have the best of two worlds.

4) When I conformed to the world, believe me, I was one of them and was accepted by them. But now that I am transformed into a new creature, they shun me because "I am different" because I place Jesus above everything. In scripture, Jesus said, "If the world hates you, keep in mind that it hated me first" (John 15:18). It's so true! And my consolation is found in Luke 6:22–23: "Blessed are ye, when men shall hate you, and when they shall separate you from their company, and shall reproach you, and cast out your name as evil, for the Son of man's sake. Rejoice ye in that day, and *leap for joy:* for, behold, *your reward is great in heaven:* for in the like manner did their fathers unto the prophets" (kjv, emphasis added).

5) The final authority for the born again experience is taken from the Word of God in the Gospel of John 3:5–7, when Jesus answered Nicodemus: "Verily, verily, I say unto thee, Except a man be born of water and *of the Spirit, he cannot enter into the kingdom of God.* That which is born of the flesh is flesh; and that which is born of the Spirit is spirit. Marvel not that I said unto thee, *Ye must be born again*" (kjv, emphasis added).

6) Also, 1 Peter 1:23: "Being born again, not of corruptible seed, but of incorruptible, by *the word of God,* which liveth and abideth for ever" (kjv, emphasis added).

To try to sum up the preceding experiences, as to why they happened—and they did happen—let me say this: God is supreme. I haven't the vaguest idea as to why all this occurred in my life after the born again experience. However, at the same time, I do recognize the fact that the enemy certainly would like to make fools of us if he can. But I also have enough faith in my Father, Abba, to know that even if I am a fool for His Son, nothing in this life really matters but for me to follow the leading of the Holy Spirit, to lift up my Savior, and to honor Almighty God with the life I now live. I am trying to live this life in the very center of God's will in accordance with the grace and light He has manifested to me. I again admit that I do not know much of anything except for the one astounding fact that *I have been born again,* and I will be with the Lord forever.

The degree of spiritual development you earnestly seek is exactly what you will attain. The decision to climb to the top of the highest mountain or to remain in the valley is yours and yours alone. No one can make that decision but you—you do have a free will. I pray through this book that God will soften your heart and you, too, will choose immortality to be in the Kingdom of God, and to worship Him in all His majesty and glory. For this you were created, and it can be yours only through being "born again."

Notes and Comments

1) Did I go bald? No! Thank God I still have the hair I had
   at the time of my conversion. My natural ash blond color
   is slowly turning gray, a beautiful "frosted" effect that I
   at one time went to the beauty salon and paid to have it
   done! Shades of wonder. God is so good! (1992)

2) After you have been born again, you have an incredibly
   intense desire to share Jesus with everyone you meet.
   The wondrous saving Gospel of Jesus must go forward
   through all believers in Jesus.

3) I had been reading a book by Sebastian Temple who was
   unendingly and feverishly seeking the "truth" as he traveled to many eastern nations; he had been actively
   involved in various religions, cults, etc., and had been
   astrally projected on many occasions. Eventually, praise
   God, he finally did find Jesus and the truth he had been
   in search of. I, too, was inquisitive (before my new glorious birth) and was practicing his type of meditation to
   achieve projection. As a result, I truly believe I had just
   a frightening foretaste of this experience. To say I was

terrified simply is not adequate. It seemed that all the forces of hell were trying to pull my soul out of my body, while at the same time, all the powers of heaven and the Holy Spirit were anchoring my soul to the unmovable Rock. The Holy Spirit won, of course. I never again attempted that type of meditation. And now I vaguely—very, very, vaguely—have a slight understanding of the G-forces the astronauts experience when they are hurtling through space with incredible speed to escape the pull of the earth's gravity. Of course, if you don't fight it and want to project astrally, your soul simply leaves your body without any problem. Readers, don't dabble or even think about it! Sebastian Temple further stated that even though he had found the truth, when he was in quiet time and meditating on the new birth, on occasion he would find himself floating without and above his physical body against his wanting to do so. *Beware—be Jesus minded* and nothing else.

4) Now, eleven years later (1992), the three tongues of fire have slowly but definitely faded from my spiritual eyes. Evidently God felt I was maturing sufficiently and the wonderful revelations, ever so subtle revelations, were no longer necessary. (A new physical baby will be weaned from its mother's milk when the proper time approaches.) Yes, it's true—I no longer needed milk; rather, I needed nourishment of meat and potatoes, so to speak, of the *Word of God.* The various lovely subtleties given to me, possibly to strengthen and encourage me—only God really knows why—were no longer necessary. I resolutely press on to further development of my spirit by studying the Holy Word of God. (1992)

5) Philippians 3:10: "I want to know Christ and the *power of his resurrection*" (emphasis added). This knowledge,

as explained in the *NIV Study Bible,* is not merely factual; it includes the experience of the *power of His resurrection.* Ephesians 1:19–20: "And his incomparably great power for us who believe. That power is like the working of his mighty strength, which he exerted in Christ when he raised him from the dead and seated him at his right hand in the heavenly realms." In these verses, Paul piles term upon term to emphasize that the *extraordinary divine force* by which Jesus Christ was raised is the *same power at work in and through believers.* I had only heard of the power of the Resurrection by the dear lady I referred to previously who had told me how Satan hated me because I now belonged to Jesus, so now Satan was tormenting me. I have read the entire Bible many, many times but had not checked the niv footnotes of Philippians 3:10 until this past year (1992). I might add that I purchased this new version only last year (1991), and I thus had this wonderful revelation. I must add that I now avidly read the footnotes where indicated. I don't want to miss a thing.

6) After dropping out of the Bible study class, I decided to do volunteer work at the VA Hospital in Bath, New York. It was a 100–mile round trip. I would be there every Sunday at 9:00 a.m. and leave at 4:00 p.m. The assignment I loved most was reading scripture to a man who was blind; he had terminal kidney problems and passed away several years later. My second duty was playing chess with a WWII soldier who was shell-shocked but amazingly could speak only the word "check-mate." My third assignment was taking wheelchair patients down from the fifth floor to the third floor where the chapel was located. I would perhaps get three or four patients down from the fifth floor before the service began. Naturally, I stayed for the service. After the service, I

would again take one patient at a time to the elevator and up to the fifth floor. I would spend the entire day at the hospital. I was faithful for perhaps nearly two years. For the first time in my life, I was beginning to learn all about "compassion and love."

Naturally Supernatural
Regeneration
Anne Fundator, Author

Endorsements

"*I* highly recommend Anne Fundator's book for reading by Christians and non-Christians alike. I found her work to be exceptionally readable. It was a delight to experience her life story and especially the unfolding of her spiritual journey. I was blessed and believe the book is anointed for ministry to spiritually hungry hearts and lives. It is my personal opinion that anyone who reads it will be touched by the Holy Spirit."

In His service,
Rev. Jeff Canankamp
Coudersport Parish, U.M.C.
December 7, 1992

"Anne's book, *Naturally Supernatural,* in manuscript form, kept me awake far into the night and I could not wait to continue reading it to the end. It is not the writing of a 'religious fanatic,' as some might think, but rather is very, very anointed writing about her experiences which were so incredibly supernatural. One can easily understand why the author is so excited and eager to share how God lifted her from the most ordinary and miserably unpleasant way of life into the heights of God's Glory.

"It is a remarkable book. The writing is excellent. The vocabulary is beautifully chosen, and Anne's childlike, enthusiastic approach is delightful. My spiritual understanding causes me to emphatically state that *God wrote the book* through Anne. No apologies are necessary for anything in it.

"For anyone who doubts that God is alive today, as in Bible times, this little book will invite their attention as surely as the desert welcomes the long awaited rain."

Thetis S. Hauber
Retired Executive Secretary
The Hypoglycemia Foundation, Inc.

"Anne Fundator states that, 'Unbelievers think if you can't see it, feel it, smell it, taste it, and hear it, it doesn't exist.' Actually, I believe many Christians have this philosophy. The ongoing spiritual battle for our hearts and souls is raging whether we know it or not, and Anne's book describes one Christian's experience in the spiritual realm. Anne honestly states that she is not certain of the source of some of her revelations—Christ or Satan. We all need to be aware of this since Satan is the great deceiver.

"We must rely on the 'Sword of the Spirit, which is the Word of God,' Ephesians 6:17, to be able to discern the spirit.

"I encourage all Christians to read this enlightening book."

Robert E. Wagner, M.D.

To Whom It May Concern:

*T*his version of *Naturally Supernatural/Regeneration* is written, copied, and printed as a "completely unedited, and unabridged version." It is not written, copied, and printed under the premise "For Sale." Therefore, the author (Anne Fundator) and R. L. Barclay (designated publication agent) are responsible for the reprinting of this publication, and have not included a bibliography, herein referring to the "fair use" concept of current copyright laws as guidelines for this action.

If at any time the material contained herein is written, copied, and published "for sale," the bibliography will be included in order to cite offerings, which might otherwise be covered under the current copyright, trademark, and patent laws.

Printed in the United States
101816LV00006B/10/A

9 781594 673009